Flags

of the World

K. L. Jott

Flags

of the World

Revised & Expanded 2nd Edition

4880 Lower Valley Road   Atglen, Pennsylvania 19310

Translated from the German by Dr. Edward Force. This book was originally published in German by Sammüller Kreativ GmbH under the title *Flaggen Dieser Welt*.
Designed by IR
Type set in Zurich BT/ITC Officina Sans

ISBN: 978-0-7643-4111-3
Printed in China

Schiffer Books are available at special discounts for bulk purchases for sales promotions or premiums. Special editions, including personalized covers, corporate imprints, and excerpts can be created in large quantities for special needs. For more information contact the publisher:

Published by Schiffer Publishing Ltd.
4880 Lower Valley Road
Atglen, PA 19310
Phone: (610) 593-1777; Fax: (610) 593-2002
E-mail: Info@schifferbooks.com

For the largest selection of fine reference books on this and related subjects, please visit our web site at **www.schifferbooks.com**
We are always looking for people to write books on new and related subjects. If you have an idea for a book please contact us at the above address.

This book may be purchased from the publisher.
Include $5.00 for shipping.
Please try your bookstore first.
You may write for a free catalog.

In Europe, Schiffer books are distributed by
Bushwood Books
6 Marksbury Ave.
Kew Gardens
Surrey TW9 4JF England
Phone: 44 (0) 20 8392 8585; Fax: 44 (0) 20 8392 9876
E-mail: info@bushwoodbooks.co.uk
Website: www.bushwoodbooks.co.uk

Contents

Preface

What is a Flag?

A flag is a symbol, made of cloth and usually rectangular, that stands for an organization or a political unit, especially, as is the subject of this book, a nation or state. Flags are now so much a part of our everyday life that we often do not notice them. Whether on television, at sporting events or demonstrations, on public buildings or ships, flags are everywhere and have a message. They express membership, whether to a team, a military unit, or a nation.

Flags have a long history, which we shall touch on briefly here. Then we shall portray over 200 flags with pictures and information on the history of the nation and its flag. Today there are 192 sovereign states recognized by the United Nations. There are also several dozen nations that now, as before, fight for the recognition of their sovereignty, and others that are still crown colonies of the former ruling powers but have attained a certain degree of self-government.

The Origin of Flags

The origins of flags and their predecessors go far back in history. Over 5000 years ago, graphic symbols were used to indicate that important personalities or even gods were present at a certain place. It is known that in the 12th century B.C. the Egyptians used cloths on poles, similar to flags, to identify the various units of their troops. Through trade and war in particular, these symbols became more and more important, and they were used more frequently to make nations recognizable.

Flags in Shipping

At sea it was especially important to recognize, even at great distances and beyond shouting distance, to whom the approaching ship belonged and whether it was friend or foe. Presumably the Vikings were the first seafarers who showed symbolic portrayals on their sails, which later were used on flags. It was also allowed in wartime to fly a neutral flag at sea to confuse the enemy. The same law, though, forbade making an attack under a false flag. When a battle was imminent, the false flag was lowered very quickly and replaced by the right one. This practice was used particularly by pirates and freebooters who sailed the seas with the intention of capturing and plundering other ships.

Almost everybody knows the Jolly Roger, the famous black flag with the white skull and crossbones. It was only one of many flags used by pirates, but its gruesome simplicity made its mark and it has become an icon of piracy.

On the high seas, flags have been used not only for mutual identification, but also for communication with signals. At the beginning of the 18th century the first signal book appeared, from which an ever-better system of generally understood signals developed in the following 150 years. Today there is a signals book with flags for every letter, and every number from 0 to 9. Every flag that represents a

letter also has a secondary meaning, such as "man overboard."

Today international regulations require that ships must show the flags of the countries in which they are registered. This is especially true of merchant ships and warships, but has also become customary for private yachts.

Flags on the Battlefield

Flags played an important role at battles on land, too, where they also served to identify the fighting troops. In addition, great numbers of military flags were developed that made the various ranks of the soldiers recognizable. To ensure that the flags of the various troops were recognizable even at great distances, the tips of the flagpoles were decorated with a so-called vexilloid, often an animal figure. The Romans already used the eagle as a vexilloid.

Flags took on special meanings during the Crusades of the European Christians, beginning in the 11th century. Most Crusader's flags bore a large cross, which also adorned their tunics. The colors of the crosses varied from country to country: The French and Spanish crusaders used red, the English white, the Italians blue. Several modern flags go back to the crusaders' flags, including, for example, those of Denmark and Britain.

Flags Today

The first modern flag was that of the Netherlands. It goes back to the 16th century and was originally orange, white, and blue. This simple horizontal tricolor became the forerunner of many similar flags.

Other flags are based on symbols of the patron saints of the countries. Britain's red right-angled cross is that of England's patron saint, St. George. The Scottish flag bears the diagonal white cross of St. Andrew.

Symbolism of the Colors

Colors are a particularly strong means of expression on present-day flags, and many colors have the same or at least a similar significance in many countries.

Red is often associated with blood, war, and sacrifice. But it also stands for courage and revolution. The color red took on a special meaning in Soviet Russia, where it stood for revolution and socialism.

White stands for purity, innocence and peace—thus being practically the opposite of red. On many flags it also symbolizes large snowy landscapes or icebergs.

Blue often stands for righteousness and, often, for peace. Sometimes it also symbolizes the sea or the sky.

Green usually represents the earth, symbolizing the fruitfulness of a land. Beyond that, green is often the color of Islam, the favorite color of the prophet Mohammed, which naturally gives it a different meaning in most Islamic lands.

Yellow often symbolizes richness, for it is the color of gold. But yellow is also the color of the sun, which it often represents.

Black is the color of Africa and often indicates the ancestry of a people. Black also often stands for a dark past and the overcoming of enemies.

Color Combinations

The combination of red, white, and blue have come to stand for freedom. The flag of the USA is based on these colors, chosen by the Continental Congress in 1777, and thus it was the first flag that represented the people more than the rulers of the land. The Stars and Stripes became the model for many other flags of countries that strove for democracy. The French Tricolor also arose out of a revolutionary movement and is the basis for many other flags around the world. The flag of Great Britain, sometimes called the Union Flag or the Union Jack, also consists of red, white and blue. In 1606, by decree, a flag design combining the red St. George's cross on a white background of the English flag with the white diagonal cross on a blue ground of the Scottish flag. In 1801 the red St. Patrick's cross of Ireland was added. The Union Jack is in the upper left canton of the British overseas territories.

The pan-African colors of red, black, green and yellow adorn many flags of independent states in Africa. They are derived from two sources: the green, yellow, and red of the Ethiopian flag, and the red, black, and green of the Universal Negro Improvement Association and African Communities League, led by Marcus Garvey. In its 1920 Declaration of Rights, these were designated as the official colors of the African race.

In many South American lands one sees variations of the Miranda flag. It takes its name from the freedom fighter Francisco de Miranda, who was one of the forerunners of the fight for freedom against the long rule by Spain and Portugal. The three equally wide stripes symbolize the separation of the New World (yellow) by the ocean (blue) from the tyranny of Spain (red).

Many Arabic lands show the same colors on their flags, often referred to as the Pan-Arab colors: black, white, green, and red. Various explanations are given, including that Mohammed used black and white banners, and that green stands for Islam. Others assert that they are ancient tribal colors or that they stand for the great deeds of the Moslems (white), the battles (black), and the swords (red), with green for the fields. Whatever their source they appeared together on the flag of the Arab Revolt in 1917.

The flag's pan-Slavic colors of red, blue, and white probably were influenced by Russia, which, in turn, may be traced to the Netherlands flag, which as noted above was the first European flag. Tsar Peter the Great was especially influenced by the clarity and simplicity of the Dutch flag and adopted the formation and colors for his merchant flag—changing only the order to white, blue and red.

Worthiness and Use of Flags

Today there is a true etiquette in the use of flags. Basically, all flags of the 192 independent countries of this world are equal—no matter whether the country is poor or rich. Consequently, flags must be set up so no country feels disadvantaged. If numerous flags are set up together, they are best arranged in a circle.

Flags must be handled with respect, since they stand for a state and its people. Many nations have established their own rules, which are not recognized internationally, for the use of their flags. Other countries, such as Great Britain, have no rules for the use of the Union Jack, although it is portrayed on several of the world's flags. The USA, on the other hand, has established a Flag Code with detailed rules for the treatment and display of its flag.

It is generally true that flags should be hoisted only from sunrise to sunset. Sometimes the times also depend on the working hours of the employees in the government buildings on which the flags are hoisted. The flags should be flown so that they fly and do not wrap around the flagstaff. The size of the flag basically depends on the event for which they are hoisted. Flags should be in good condition, not faded or torn.

One often sees flags flying at half-mast. This is done for national mourning or a state funeral. Many countries also give the flag a mourning symbol or have it bound so it cannot fly.

Flags of Organizations and in Sports

Internationally active organizations, such as the UN, NATO, and the EU, and non-political organizations like the Red Cross also have flags to indicate their presence in a country or their internal meetings. The most famous flag in sports is surely the Olympic flag, which was designed in 1914. The white ground symbolizes peace and brotherly association. The blue ring stands for Europe, the black for Africa, the red for America, the yellow for Asia and the green for Australia.

In sports banners and flags have long been used as logos for the teams. Today, every soccer team has its own flag, and recently flags in stadiums have become a clear indication of a strongly felt allegiance.

GREENLAND

ICELAND

FAROE ISLANDS

NORWAY

SWEDEN

FINLAND

ESTONIA

RUSSIA

LATVIA

LITHUANIA

DENMARK

IRELAND

UNITED
KINGDOM

NETHERLANDS

BELARUS

BELGIUM

GERMANY

POLAND

LUXEMBOURG

CZECH REPUBLIC

UKRAINE

LIECHTENSTEIN

SLOVAKIA

FRANCE

MOLDOVA

SWITZERLAND

AUSTRIA

HUNGARY

SLOVENIA

ROMANIA

CROATIA

PORTUGAL

ANDORRA

SAN MARINO

BOSNIA
HERZEGOVINA

SERBIA

BULGARIA

VATICAN
CITY

SPAIN

MONTENEGRO

MACEDONIA

ITALY

GIBRALTAR

ALBANIA

GREECE

MALTA

CYPRESS

Europe, because of its historical development, is regarded as an individual continent, although strictly speaking it is a subcontinent of Asia.

Europe is the second-smallest continent, with 10.5 million square kilometers. With 730 million population, it ranks third after Asia and Africa. 75% of the population is Christian, about 8% Moslem. Europe consists of 44 independent states; the largest is Russia, the smallest the Vatican City. The largest city is Moscow, with 14.4 million population.

Europe was influenced above all by the Greek culture, the Roman Empire, and Christianity.

In the 20th century great changes took place in Europe. Through two world wars, the rise and fall of Communism, the tendency toward individual states and the counter-movement of the European Union, which wants to establish an economic union. Since 1990 the number of independent states in Europe has risen from 34 to 44.

There is no natural boundary between Europe and Asia, and drawing a boundary line has often been discussed. Today it is defined by the Ural Mountains, Ural River, Caspian Sea and Sea of Azov, and for Asia Minor the Black Sea and the Bosporus. Only a quarter of Russia is in Europe, but since this quarter is the historical nucleus and 75% of the population lives there, you will find Russia in the Europe chapter.

red dots on the maps indicate capital cities

EUROPE

EUROPE

Albania

Republic of Albania

Capital: Tirana
Area: 28,748 sq. km.
Population: 3,000,000
Languages: Albanian
(official), Greek,
Macedonian

Currency: Lek
Member: OSCE, UN
Economy: Petroleum,
metals, farm produce,
textiles and shoes

Native name: Shqipëria (Albanian)
German: Albanien
French: Albanie
Spanish: Albania

A black double eagle was the family emblem of the national hero, Gjergj Skanderbeg, who led the fight for freedom from the Turks in the 15th century. This eagle, on a red ground, still adorns the Albanian flag today. According to a legend, the Albanians themselves are descended from eagles. After World War II the Communist star was placed above the eagle, but it was removed in 1992, when the flag was introduced in its present form.

Andorra

Principality of Andorra

Capital: Andorra la Vella
Area: 467.76 sq. km.
Population: 85,000
Languages: Catalan
(official), Spanish,
French
Currency: Euro

Member: OSCE, UN
Economy: Mainly
tourism; export goods
are transport devices,
optical and other
instruments; main
export country is Spain.

Native name: Andorra (Catalan)
German: Andorra
French: Andorre
Spanish: Andorra

Andorra ranks among the world's oldest states. Its flag originally had a yellow and a red stripe, in reference to the arms of the counts of Foix and their heirs, the counts of Béarn. In 1866, Napoleon III added the blue stripe. The fields in the arms stand for the lords of the land: the bishop's mitre for the Bishop of Urgel, three bars for the Bishop of Foix, four bars for Catalonia and the cows for the counts of Béarn.

Austria

Republic of Austria

Capital: Vienna
Area: 83,871 sq. km.
Population: 8,220,000
Languages: German,
(regionally Slovenian,
Croatian, Hungarian)
Currency: Euro

Member: EU, OECD,
OSCE, UN, WEU
(observer)
Economy: Main exports
are finished goods
(machines and motor
vehicles)

After World War I, Austria took up the red-white-red colors whose origins lie far back in time; a legend says that the white robe of a duke was saturated with blood in combat. When he removed his sword belt, a white stripe remained to be seen. This flag was already a sea battle flag in 1786. It was introduced as the national flag only after World War I and again after World War II.

Native name: Österreich (German)
French: Autriche
Spanish: Austria

Austrian Federal States

Burgenland

Area: 3,965 sq. km.
Population: 277,569
Capital: Eisenstadt
A golden shield with a red eagle on the red-gold colors of Burgenland.

Carinthia (Kämten)

Area: 9,535 sq. km.
Population: 559,404
Capital: Klagenfurt
Three lions, one above another, on the shield. The Hapsburgs have used these arms since 1335.

Lower Austria

(Niederösterreich)
Area: 19,178 sq. km.
Population: 1,545,804
Capital: St. Pölten
Five golden eagles on a blue shield. The five-eagle arms first appeared in 1335.

EUROPE

Salzburg
Area: 7,154 sq. km.
Population: 521,238
Capital: Salzburg
A split shield with lion and a princely crown on top. The arms originated 1284-90.

Styria (Steiermark)
Area: 16,388 sq. km.
Population: 1,183,303
Capital: Graz
A panther on the shield, below the ducal hat of Styria crown. Known to exist since 1246.

Tyrol (Tirol)
Area: 12,648 sq. km.
Population: 360,168
Capital: Innsbruck
The arms show an eagle with golden arms. This form dates from 1340.

Upper Austria (Oberösterreich)
Area: 11,980 sq. km.
Population: 1,376,797
Capital: Linz
The Austrian archducal crown, split shield with eagle. The arms date from 1390.

Vienna (Wien)
Area: 415 sq. km.
Population: 1,631,082
Capital: Vienna
A white cross on a red shield; can also bear a black eagle.

Vorarlberg
Area: 2,601 sq. km.
Population: 686,80,9
Capital: Breganz
The shield bears a red church flag and is known to exist since 1181.

Belarus

Republic of Belarus
Capital: Minsk
Area: 207,595 sq. km.
Population: 9,578,000
Languages: Belarusian, Russian
Currency: Belarus Rubel

Member: GUS, OSCE, UN
Economy: Exported are raw minerals, machines, vehicles,chemical and plastic products

Native name: Byelarus
German: Weissrussland
French: Biélorussie
Spanish: Belorrusia

When Belarus became independent in 1991, the traditional red-white-red flag was used, but in 1995 the flag was changed to its present form. It is a modification of its 1951 flag when the country was a republic of the Soviet Union. The narrow band portrays a woven cloth in the pattern of the national costume. Red stands for socialism, green for agriculture and forests.

Belgium

Kingdom of Belgium
Capital: Brussels
Area: 32,545 sq. km.
Population: 10,430,000
Languages: Flemish, French, German
Currency: Euro
Membership: EU, NATO, OECD, OSCE, UN, WEU

Economy: Export and import concentrate strongly on the other EU countries. Most important trade goods: chemical products, metals and metal goods, machines and equipment

The Belgian flag is a vertical tricolor based on the French flag, but the colors come from those of the provinces of Brabant (a lion on black ground), Flanders (a lion on golden ground) and Hennegau (black and red lions on gold). The flag was introduced in 1830 when the independent kingdom of Belgium was founded, but had already flown in 1792 during rebellions against the Hapsburg overlords.

Native name: Belgie (Flemish)
German: Belgien
French: Belgique
Spanish: Bélgica

Bosnia and Herzegovina

Bosnia and Herzegovina
Capital: Sarajevo
Area: 51,197 sq. km.
Population: 4,622,000
Languages: Bosnian, Croatian, Serbian
Currency: Convertible Mark

Member: OSCE. UN
Economy: Economic life is still limited by the war. Exports are manufactured and finished goods, raw materials and machines.

The flag of Bosnia and Herzegovina was introduced through the UN Security Council in February 1998. The colors of dark blue and yellow and the stars are taken from the European flag. The yellow triangle symbolizes the shape of the country, as well as the three ethnic groups: Bosniaks, Serbs, and Croats. The two districts of Bosniak-Croatian Federation (51%) and Serbian Republic (49%) have their own state flags.

Native name: Bosna I Hercegovina
(Bosnian, Croatian)
German: Bosnien und Herzegovina
French: Bosnie-Herzégovine
Spanish: Bosnia y Herzegovina

EUROPE

Bulgaria

Native name: Republika Balgariya
German: Bulgarien
French: Bulgarie
Spanish: Bulgaria

Republic of Bulgaria
Capital: Sofia
Area: 110,994 sq. km.
Population: 7,093,000
Language: Bulgarian
Currency: Leva

Member: NATO, OSCE, UN, WEU (assoc. partner)
Economy: Machines, semi-manufactured goods, tobacco, wine, chemicals

In 1908 Bulgaria became an independent kingdom. In 1945 the monarchy was abolished and a people's republic proclaimed. The white stripe was temporarily adorned with a lion, the Red Star and a gear wheel. After the break with Communism in 1990 these symbols were removed. White stands for love of peace and work, green for the fruitfulness of the soil and loyalty to the homeland, and red for the bravery of the people.

Croatia

Native name: Republika Hrvatska
German: Republik Kroatien
French: Croatie
Spanish: Croacia

Republic of Croatia
Capital: Zagreb
Area: 56,542 sq. km.
Population: 4,483,000
Language: Croatian
Currency: Kuna

Member: OSCE, UN
Economy: Fuels and lubricants, chemicals, foods and means of entertainment

The shield in the center of the Croatian flag has been the arms of Croatia since the 16th century. The crown on the shield consists of five different coats of arms, standing for the Croatian regions of Old Croatia, Dubrovnik, Dalmatia, Istria and Slavonia. During the Communist era the crown was replaced by a red star. But when Croatia attained independence and became a republic in 1991, the flag was introduced again in its traditional form.

Cyprus

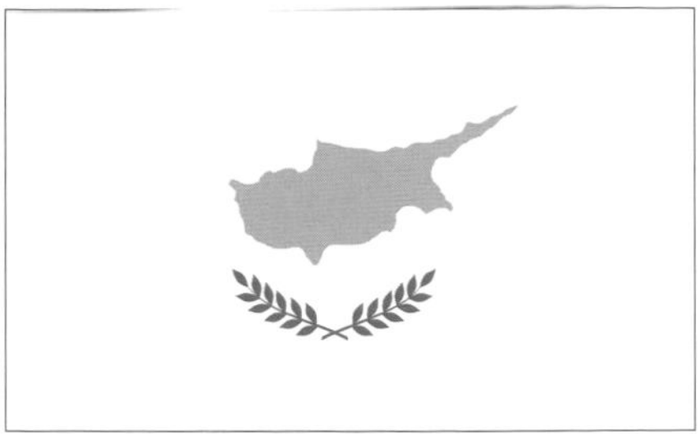

Republic of Cyprus
Capital: Nicosia
Area: 9,251 sq. km.
Population: 1,120,000
Languages: Greek, Turkish
Currency: Cyprus Pound
Member: EU (Greek part), OSCE, UN
Economy: Industrial and agricultural products

The white ground of the national flag and the olive branch stand for the peaceful co-existence of the Greek and Turkish Cypriots. The island itself is shown in gold and refers to the copper deposits that gave the island its name (kypros = copper). Since the division, this flag is seen only in the Greek part of the island. In the Turkish north a version of the Turkish national flag is used. The "Turkish Republic of North Cyprus" is recognized only by Turkey.

Native name: Kypriaki Dimokratia (Greek), Kibris Cumhuriyeti (Turkish)
German: Zypern
French: Chypre
Spanish: Chipre

Czech Republic

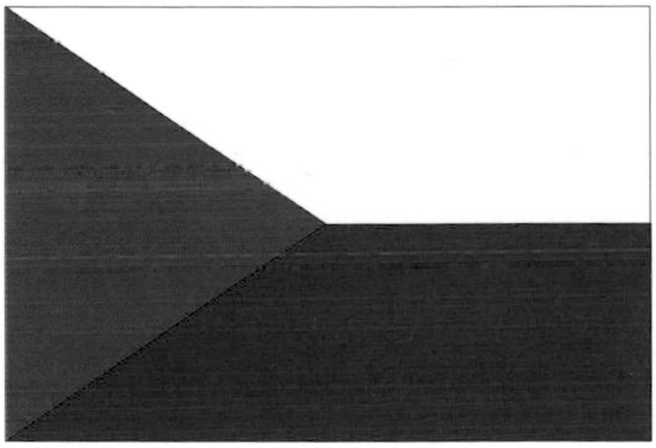

Czech Republic
Capital: Prague
Area: 78,866 sq. km.
Population: 10,190,000
Language: Czech
Currency: Czech Krone
Member: EU, NATO, OECD, OSCE, UN, WEU (associate)
Economy: Machinery, vehicles and their parts are exported

The Czech Republic, when Czechoslovakia was separated into it and Slovakia in 1993, took over the flag, while Slovakia gained a new flag. Blue, white and red are the pan-Slavic colors, and white and red are the traditional colors of Bohemia, while blue is the color of Moravia. The flag was first introduced for Czechoslovakia in 1920.

Native name: Cesko Republika
German: Tschechien
French: République techèque
Spanish: República Checa

Denmark

Kingdom of Denmark
Capital: Copenhagen
Area: 43,096 sq. km.
Population: 5,529,000
Language: Danish
Currency: Danish Krone

Member: EU, NATO,
OECD, UN, WEO
(observer)
Economy: Ship, factory
and machinery building

Native name: Kongeriget Danmark
German: Dänemark
French: Danemark
Spanish: Dinamarka

The flag of Denmark is presumably the oldest national flag on earth. According to a legend, King Waldemar II saw the "Dannebrog" (Danish cloth) fall from heaven during a battle against the Estonians in 1219. Encouraged by it, the Danes won the battle. The basic pattern may be based on the red battle flag with the white cross of Christianity. Originally the cross divided the flag into four equally large parts; only later was the vertical bar moved. The external territories of the Faroes and Greenland have their own flags.

Estonia

Republic of Estonia
Capital: Tallinn
Area: 45,227 sq. km.
Population: 1,283,000
Language: Estonian
Currency: Estonian Krone

Member: EU, NATO,
OSCE, UN, WEU
(observer)
Economy: Animal
agriculture, fishing

Native name: Eesti Vabariik
German: Estland
French: Estonie
Spanish: Estonia

The Estonian flag was brought into existence by a student movement in 1881 and made the national flag in 1918, when Estonia gained independence from Russia. The blue stripe stands for the sky and loyalty, the black for the dark soil of the country and the farmers' traditional black clothing. The white stripe stands for snow and symbolizes the wish for peace and freedom.

Faroe Islands

Faroe Islands

Capital: Thórshavn
Area: 1,398.9 sq. km.
Population: 48,353
Languages: Faeroese, Danish

Currency: Kronur
Possessor: Denmark
Economy: Main exports are ships, fish and fish products

The Faroes consist of 18 islands, 17 of them populated. Since 1948 they have been an autonomous region with their own parliament and two delegates to the Danish parliament. The Population are descended from the Vikings. The islands have belonged to Denmark since the 14th century. The form of the flag and the cross are based on the Norwegian flag. A red cross outlined in blue stands on a white ground. Red and blue are traditional colors of the Faroese; white stands for the sky and the ocean waves.

Native name: Føroyar
German: Färöer
French: Iles Féroé
Spanish: Islas Feroe

Finland

Republic of Finland

Capital: Helsinki
Area: 338,144 sq. km.
Population: 5,259,000
Languages: Finnish, Swedish
Currency: Euro

Member: EU, OECD, OSCE,UN, WEU (observer)
Economy: Wood, optical equipment, paper and paper products

The white ground color of the Finnish flag symbolizes the vast snowy landscapes and the blue stands for the sky and the many lakes (over 60,000!). Before the flag was introduced in its present form in 1918, it had several variations, always based on the colors of blue and white. The form of the cross indicates Finland's being one of the Nordic states.

Native name: Suomen tasavalta (Finnish), Republiken Finland, Finland (Swedish)
German: Finnland
French: Finlande
Spanish: Finlandia

EUROPE

France

French Republic
Capital: Paris
Area: 643,965 sq. km.
Population: 65,312,000
Language: French
Currency: Euro

Member: EU, G-8, NATO, OECD, OSCE, UN, WEU
Economy: Tourism, semi-finished products, consumer goods, foods

Native name: Republique francaise
Native language: France
German: Frankreich
Spanish: Francia

The French tricolor has existed since 1848. Red and blue are the colors of Paris, white is the color of the house of Bourbon and is linked with both the Virgin Mary and the national heroine Joan of Arc. In addition, the colors stand for the goals of the French Revolution: liberty, equality and fraternity. In France, the color combination was formed for the first time during the French Revolution.

Germany

Federal Republic of Germany
Capital: Berlin
Area: 357,030 sq. km.
Population: 81,471,000
Language: German
Currency: Euro

Member: EU, G-8, NATO, OECD, OSCE, UN, WEU
Economy: Autos and parts, machines, chemical products, electronics

Native name: Deutschland
English: Germany
French: Allemagne
Spanish: Alemania

The colors of the German tricolor are based on the uniforms of the soldiers in the times of the Wars of Liberation (black uniforms with red piping and yellow buttons). In the Middle Ages the German flag colors had been black and yellow and red and white. When the Reich was founded in 1871 the first German national flag was black, white and red. The Weimar Republic officially introduced the black-red-gold colors after World War I. Since 1949 this tricolor has been the German flag. The 16 federal states all have their own state flags.

Flag of the German Reich (1871-1918)
It was introduced by Bismarck in 1867. Black and white were the colors of Prussia, red the color of Brandenburg.

Federal Service Flag
Along with the national flag (above), the service flag of the German federal offices still exists. It is a symbol of the federation and may be used only by federal institutions.

Flag of the German Democratic Republic from 1949 to 1989. In 1950 the emblem of hammer, compass and circling sheaves of wheat was placed in the center. This emblem resembled that on the flag of the Soviet Union.

The Federal States of Germany

Baden-Württemberg
Area: 35,751 sq .km.
Population: 10,717,419
Capital: Stuttgart

The black and yellow flag of Baden-Württemberg was introduced in 1952. The colors are based on those of the states of Baden (yellow and red) and Württemberg (black and red) and the emblem of the house of Staufen, showing three black lions on a golden ground. Swabia was the home area of the ruling house of Staufen.

Bayern –
Free State of Bavaria
Area: 70,549 sq. km.
Population: 12,443,893
Capital: München
(Munich)

The colors of white (or silver) and blue were the colors of the house of Wittelsbach and of Bavaria since the beginning of the 12th century. The diamond pattern is also known since the 12th century. It comes from the heraldry of the Counts of Bogen. The Bavarian state flag exists in a form with stripes and one with diamonds.

EUROPE

Berlin
Area: 891 sq. km.
Population: 3,387,828

The Berlin flag shows a black bear on a white shield. The bear was first immortalized on a seal in 1280. Presumably the choice of a bear goes back to Albrecht the Bear, who founded the Mark Brandenburg in the 12th century. Above and below the white stripe are red stripes; red and white are the traditional colors of Brandenburg.

Brandenburg
Area: 29,477 sq. km.
Population: 2,567,704
Capital: Potsdam

The state colors of Brandenburg are taken from the arms of the former ruling family (Electors of Brandenburg). The eagle presumably goes back to Otto I, the son of the founder of Brandenburg. It is presumably based on the German royal eagle.

Bremen – Free Hansa City of Bremen
Area: 404 sq. km.
Population: 663,213

The red and white flag of Bremen is based on the colors of the arms of Bremen and the colors of the Hanseatic League. Ships from Bremen took them from the colors of the empire's battle flag: a white cross on a red ground. Since 1336 the arms show the key of St. Peter, Bremen's patron saint.

Hamburg – Free Hansa City Hamburg
Area: 755 sq. km.
Population: 1,734,830

The flag of the free Hansa city of Hamburg shows a white castle on a red ground. The castle is either the Hammaburg, built by Charlemagne in 808, or shows the fortified city with the tower of the cathedral, which is dedicated to the Virgin Mary. This castle was already shown on a seal in 1241.

Hessen
Area: 21,114 sq. km.
Population: 6,097,765
Capital: Wiesbaden

The colors of red and white are based on those of the Archbishopric of Mainz. The lion was originally the armorial animal of Thuringia, to which margravate Hesse belonged until 1247.

Mecklenburg-Vorpommern
Area: 23,174 sq. km.
Population: 1,719,653
Capital: Schwerin

The flag is colored blue, white, yellow and red. Blue and white stand for Pomerania, blue, yellow and red are the colors of Mecklenburg. The oxhead has been on the arms of Mecklenburg since the 13th century; the griffin is the armorial animal of the dukes of Pomerania.

Niedersachsen
Area: 47,618 sq. km.
Population: 8,000,909
Capital: Hannover

The flag shows the German tricolor with a red shield on which a white horse stands. The white horse (Saxon horse of the Guelphs) comes from the arms of the dukes of Braunschweig. In 1949 it was decided to underlay the arms with the colors of the federal flag, since a combination of the traditional state colors would have made a gaudy flag.

Nordrhein-Westfalen
Area: 34,083 sq. km.
Population: 18,075,352
Capital: Düsseldorf

The flag colors, green, white and red, are based on the colors of the former Prussian province of Rhineland (green and white) and Westphalia (red and white). They are also found in the arms, which shows a shield in these colors. The left half symbolizes the Rhineland, the horse at right stands for Westphalia. The rose comes from the arms of the princes of Lippe.

Rheinland-Pfalz
Area: 19,847 sq. km.
Population: 4,061,105
Capital: Mainz

The flag shows the German tricolor with arms at the upper left. The colors of black, red and gold derive from the arms of Rheinland-Pfalz. The arms combine those of three medieval electoral states: The red cross stands for the former Electorate of Trier, the white wheel for the Archbishopric of Mainz, and the golden lion for the Counts Palatine.

Saarland
Area: 2,568 sq. km.
Population: 1,056,417
Capital: Saarbrücken

The flag of Saarland is also black-red-gold, with its special features in the coat of arms. Each part of the arms shows the heraldic symbol of a former part of the state: the silver lion stands for Nassau-Saarbrücken, the cross for Trier, the golden lion for Pfalz-Zweibrücken and the eagle for Lorraine.

**Sachsen –
Free State of Saxony**
Area: 18,413 sq. km.
Population: 4,296,284
Capital: Dresden

White and green are the traditional colors of Saxony. The gold and black bars on the shield come from the arms of Anhalt. The wreath was originally a laurel wreath and comes from the arms of the Saxon dukes in the 13th century.

Sachsen-Anhalt
Area: 20,445 sq. km.
Population: 2,494,437
Capital: Magdeburg

The gold and black colors originated on the medieval Saxon coat of arms. In the center of the flag is a coat of arms divided in two: The upper field shows the arms of Saxony, with the Prussian eagle in the upper right corner. The lower half shows the arms of the free state of Anhalt of 1924.

Schleswig-Holstein
Area: 15,763 sq. km.
Population: 2,828,760
Capital: Kiel

The blue-white-red colors come from the state colors of blue and yellow for the duchy of Schleswig and white and red for Holstein. The two blue lions come from the Danish arms; the Holstein nettle leaf presumably from the arms of the Schauenburger.

Thüringen –
Free State of Thuringia
Area: 16,172 sq. km.
Population: 2,355,280
Capital: Erfurt

The white and red flag colors exist since 1920, when Thuringia was created out of several small states. A lion has adorned the arms of the landgraves of Thuringia since the 13th century. The eight stars on the shield represents the united lands in the founding year and the formerly Prussian areas that were added in 1945.

Gibraltar

British Crown Colony of Gibraltar
Capital: City of Gibraltar
Area: 6.5 sq. km.
Population: 28,925
Languages: English, Spanish

Currency: Gibraltar Pound
Belongs to: Great Britain
Economy: Mainly tourism, also shipfitting

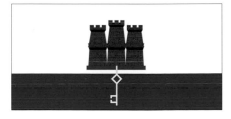

Gibraltar has the status of "British Overseas Territory." It has belonged to Britain since 1713 and was a British colony since 1830. Gibraltar has its own parliament with a governor and a head of government. The flag of Gibraltar has a wide white stripe and a narrow red one under it. On the white stripe is a castle with three towers; on the red stripe is a gold key. The castle stands for the security of Gibraltar, the key for access to the Mediterranean Sea.

Native name: Gibraltar (English)
German: Gibraltar
French: Gibraltar
Spanish: Gibraltar

EUROPE

Greece

Hellenic Republic
Capital: Athens
Area: 131,957 sq. km.
Population: 10,760,000
Language: Greek
Currency: Euro

Member: EU, NATO, OECD, OSCE, UN, WEU
Economy: Finished products, foods, machines, vehicles

Native name: Elliniki Dhimokratia
German: Griechenland
French: Grèce
Spanish: Grecia

The Greek flag symbolizes the Greek struggle for independence against the Ottoman Empire. The nine horizontal stripes stand for the nine syllables of the Greek battle cry: "Eleutheria e Thanatos" (Liberty or Death). The color blue also stands for the sea and sky, the color white for the purity of the fight for liberty. The cross stands for God's wisdom, freedom and the land. It shows Greece's link with the Orthodox church. The flag was confirmed in its present form in 1873.

Greenland

Greenland
Capital: Nuuk
Area: 2,166,086 sq. km.
Population: 57,670
Languages: Greenlandic, Danish
Currency: Danish Krone

Belongs to: Denmark
Economy: Fishing dominates; the main export is fish

Native name: Kalaallit Nunaat (Kalaal-lisut), Grønland (Danish)
German: Grönland
French: Groenland
Spanish: Groenlandia

Since 1943 Greenland, the world's largest island, has been an equal part of Denmark; since 1959 it has had internal autonomy. Greenland has its own parliament plus two delegates to the Danish parliament. The flag is red and white like the Danish flag. The white stripe stands for the icecap, the white semicircle for the icebergs. The red stripe represents the ocean, the red semicircle the fjords. Together the semicircles symbolize the sun.

Hungary

Republic of Hungary

Capital: Budapest
Area: 93,030 sq. km.
Population: 9,976,000
Language: Hungarian
Currency: Forint
Member: EU, NATO,
OECD, OSCE, UN, WEU
(associate)
Economy:
Telecommunications
and audio equipment,
vehicles, metals

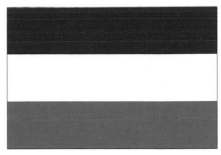

The colors of the flag presumably come from the medieval arms of Hungary. The stripe design was borrowed from the French tricolor. When Hungary fought against Austrian rule in 1848, a red-white-green tricolor was hoisted. Red stands for strength, white for awareness of duty, and green for hope. The flag was introduced in 1957.

Native name: Magyar Kozlarsasay
German: Ungarn
French: Hongrie
Spanish: Hungria

Iceland

Republic of Iceland

Capital: Reykjavik
Area: 103,000 sq. km.
Population: 311,000
Language: Icelandic
Currency: Icelandic
Krone
Member: NATO,
OECD, OSCE, UN, WEU
(associate)
Economy: Fish and fish
products, aluminum,
medicines

The blue and white colors stand for the sea and ice, and were already immortalized in the traditional clothing of the Icelanders. Only later was the red of Denmark added, for Iceland was under Danish occupation since the 14th century. The form of the cross indicates membership in the Nordic family of peoples. Since 1944 Iceland has been an independent republic. In the same year the flag was officially introduced.

Native name: Lydveldid Island
German: Island
French: Islande
Spanish: Islandia

EUROPE

Ireland

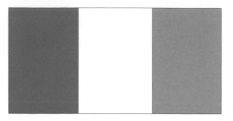

Republic of Ireland
Capital: Dublin
Area: 70,273 sq. km.
Population: 4,670,000
Languages: Irish, English
Currency: Euro

Member: EU, OPEC, UN
Economy: Chemical products, machines and transportation equipment

Native name: Eire (Irish)
German: Irland
French: Irlande
Spanish: Irlanda

Green was always the color of the island; it stands for both the Gallic and the Norman tradition, and is also the traditional color of the Catholics. In the freedom fighting of the Irish nationalists against Great Britain, orange and white were used along with green; orange stood for the Protestant minority, the political adherents of William of Orange. White stands for unity and peaceful cooperation of the two religions.

Italy

Italian Republic
Capital: Rome
Area: 301,399 sq. km.
Population: 61,016,000
Languages: Italian, (regionally German, French, Slovenian)
Currency: Euro

Member: EU, G-8, NATO, OECD, OSCE, UN, WEU
Economy: Tourism, main exports are machines, production lines, motor vehicles, clothing, wine

Native name: Repubblica Italiana (Italia)
German: Italien
French: Italie
Spanish: Italia

The model for the Italian flag was the French tricolor, and when Italy was under French rule from 1796 to 1814, the flag was created, apparently by Napoleon. The colors come from the uniforms of the state militia of Milan and the so-called "Italian Legion" (a local home guard of Modena). From 1861 to 1946 the arms of the royal house of Savoy adorned the flag. When Italy became a republic in 1946, the arms disappeared.

Latvia

Republic of Latvia
Capital: Riga
Area: 64,589 sq. km.
Population: 2,205,000
Language: Latvian
Currency: Lats
Member: EU, NATO, OSCE, UN, WEU

(associate)
Economy: Export of wood and wood products, metals, machines and textiles, 77% to other EU countries

In the 13th century, a flag similar to the present one was already used by Lettish tribes. The present flag was designed at the end of the 19th century and used until 1940. Then Latvia was annexed by the Soviet Union and the flag was banned. The white middle stripe stands for the justice, faith, and honor of the land's free citizens. The dark red color stands for the blood that was shed before Latvia finally won its freedom.

Native name: Latvijas Republika
    (Latvija)
German: Lettland
French: Lettonie
Spanish: Letonia

Liechtenstein

Principality of Liechtenstein
Capital: Vaduz
Area: 160 sq. km.
Population: 35,000
Language: German
Currency: Swiss Franc

Member: OSCE, UN
Economy: Ecxports are machines, electronic products, metal goods, glassware, ceramics

The blue color symbolizes the sky, while the red stands for the glow of the earth and the mountains in the evening. The golden crown in the blue stripe was introduced in 1937, after it was found at the 1936 Olympic Games that the flags of Liechtenstein and Haiti were identical. The crown indicates that the land is a principality, but also symbolizes the unity of the people, princely house and government.

Native name: Fuerstentum Liechten-
    stein (Liechtenstein)
German: Liechtenstein
French: Liechtenstein
Spanish: Liechtenstein

EUROPE

Lithuania

Republic of Lithuania
Capital: Vilnius
Area: 65,301 sq. km.
Population: 3,500,000
Language: Lithuanian
Currency: Litas
Member: EU, NATO,
OSCE, UN, WEU
(associate)
Economy: Finished
goods, kitchen utensils,
machines, chemical
products

Native name: Lietuvos Respublika
(Lietuva)
German: Litauen
French: Lituanie
Spanish: Lituania

The present flag of Lithuania is a horizontal
tricolor of yellow, green and red. After the country
had been freed from Russian rule in 1918, after
World War I, this flag was used until the country
was occupied by Russia again in 1940 and the flag
was banned. Only in 1989 was it introduced again.
The yellow stands for the waving fields of grain,
the green symbolizes the many forests and the life
of the country. Red stands for Lithuania's rich
flora, but also for the blood that was shed in the
battles for the country's sovereignty.

Luxembourg

Grand Duchy of
Luxembourg
Capital: Luxembourg
Area: 2,586 sq. km.
Population: 503,000
Languages:Luxembourgish,
German, French
Currency: Euro
Member: EU, NATO,
OECD, OSCE, UN, WEU
Economy: Iron and steel
goods, machines and
equipment

Native name: Grand Duche de Luxem-
bourg (Luxembourg)
German: Luxemburg
Spanish: Luxemburgo

The colors of the flag of Luxembourg are based on
the colors of the arms of a grand duke of the 13th
century. At the beginning of the 19th century
Luxembourg was part of the Netherlands; thus the
similarity of design and colors of the flags. The
blue of the flag of Luxembourg is lighter than that
of the Netherlands. The flag was introduced in its
present form in 1845.

Macedonia

Republic of Macedonia

Capital: Skopje
Area: 25,713 sq. km.
Population: 2,049,000
Languages: Macedonian, Albanian
Currency: Denar

Economy: Finished goods, drinks, tobacco, foods, livestock

For centuries the country was under Turkish rule; from 1913 to 1919 it belonged to Serbia, then it became part of Yugoslavia. During the 1945-1991 Communist regime, the flag bore a red star with a gold border on a red ground. In 1991 the flag with a 16-cornered star was introduced, against which Greece protested. Since 1995 the Macedonian flag shows a yellow sun with eight rays. The sun stands for light, life, happiness and freedom. Red is the country's national color.

Native name: Republika Makedonija (Macedonian), Maqedonia (Albanian)
German: Mazedonien
French: Macédonie
Spanish: Macedonia

Malta

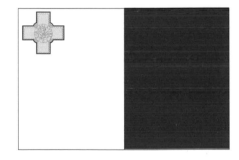

Republic of Malta

Capital: Valletta
Area: 315.6 sq/km.
Population: 408,000
Languages: Maltese, English
Currency: Maltese Lira

Member: EU, OSCE, UN
Economy: Machines and means of transportation, tourism

The colors of red and white are those of the Knights of St. John, which made the island their headquarters in 1530. They defended the island successfully against the Turks until 1565. As of 1800 Malta was a British fleet support point; it was strategically important during World War II. Because of the brave resistance of the Maltese, Britain awarded them the Cross of St. George in 1942; since then it has stood in the upper corner of the flag.

Native name: Repubblika ta' Malta (Malta)
German: Malta
French: Malte
Spanish: Malta

EUROPE

Moldova

Republic of Moldova
Capital: Chisinau
Area: 33,800 sq. km.
Population: 4,314,000
Languages: Moldavian, Romanian
Currency: Moldau-Leu

Member: GUS, OSCE, UN
Economy: Textiles, leather goods, foods

Native name: Republica Moldova
(Moldova)
German: Moldawien
French: Moldavie
Spanish: Moldavia

The flag of Moldova was introduced in 1990, In 1940 Moldova was taken into the Soviet Union, and at its dissolution the separatist movement turned toward Romania. Thus the colors and eagle on the flag go back to the Romanian flag and arms. The shield shows a golden eagle with a cross in its beak and an olive branch and St. Michael's scepter in its claws. The shield portrays traditional symbols of Moldova: the ox head, rose, half-moon and star.

Monaco

Principality of Monaco
Capital: Monaco-Ville
Area: 1.95 sq. km.
Population: 31,000
Language: French
Currency: Euro

Member: OSCE, UN
Economy: Tourism, banking, sevices.
Highest per capita gross national product in the world

Native name: Principaute de Monaco
(Monaco)
German: Monaco
Spanish: Monaco

Monaco is the world's second smallest country (after Vatican City). The flag of two equal stripes in red and white is based on the colors of the princely Grimaldi family, which has ruled the principality for over 700 years. The flag was introduced in 1881.

Montenegro

Montenegro
Capital: Podgorica
Area: 13,812 sq. km.
Population: 661,000
Languages: Serbian, Albanian
Currency: Euro

Economy: Bauxite and iron ores, brown coal, tobacco, salt products. Agrarian economy with vegetables, grain, potatoes, wine, citrus fruit

In May 2006, the population decided in a first plebiscite for independence from the union of Serbia and Montenegro. The Montenegrin flag, which was accepted on July 12, 2004, goes back to the historic flag that was used until World War I, the time of the first Montenegrin independence. The golden lion on the eagle's shield is an old Montenegrin national symbol.

Native name: Crna Gora (Serbian)
German: Montenegro
French: Monténégro
Spanish: Montenegro

Netherlands

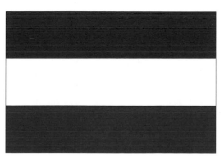

Kingdom of the Netherlands
Capital: Amsterdam
Area: 41,526 sq. km.
Population: 16,800,000
Language: Hollands ("Dutch")
Currency: Euro

Member: EU, NATO, OECD, OSCE, UN, WEU
Economy: Export-intensive agriculture with vegetables, flowers and cattle. 20% of the exports go to Germany.

The Netherlands have the oldest tricolor in the world; it is known since 1579. At first the upper stripe was orange, based on the colors of Prince Willem of Orange-Nassau, who fought for freedom against Spain. White and blue are the colors of Nassau. In 1796, the orange stripe was changed to red to be better recognizable at sea. But orange is still the color of the royal house, and on special days an orange triangular flag is hoisted over the tricolor.

Native name: Koninkrijk der Nederlan-den (Nederland)
German: Niederlande
French: Pays-Bas
Spanish: Paises Bajos

EUROPE

Norway

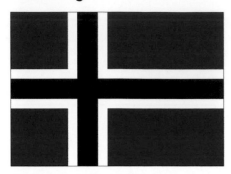

Native name: Kongeriket Norge
(Norge)
German: Norwegen
French: Norvège
Spanish: Noruega

Kingdom of Norway
Capital: Oslo
Area: 323,759 sq. km.
Population: 4,690,000
Language: Norwegian
Currency: Norwegian
Krone

Member: NATO,
OECD, OSCE, UN, WEU
(associate)
Economy: Petroleum,
natural gas,
petrochemicals

From 1380 to 1814 Norway was under Danish rule. In 1814 Denmark had to give Norway to Sweden. Since 1821 Norway has had its own flag, with the blue cross added to the Danish flag. Norway had to fight a long time before its flag was also accepted by Sweden. Only in 1905 did the union with Sweden end. The cross form is typical of the Nordic lands.

Poland

Native name: Rzeczpospolita Polska
(Polska)
German: Polen
French: Pologne
Spanish: Polonia

Republic of Poland
Capital: Warsaw
Area: 312,685 sq. km.
Population: 38,440,000
Language: Polish
Currency: Zloty
Member: EU, NATO,

OECD, OSCE, UN, WEU
(associate)
Economy: Main exports
are machines and
electric equipment, also
chemical and plastic
products.

The red and white colors had already appeared in military uniforms at the beginning of the 13th century. But only in 1831 did they become the national colors. The colors are also found on the national coat of arms with a silver eagle on a red background. The stripes are equally wide.

Portugal

Portuguese Republic
Capital: Lisbon
Area: 92,345 sq. km.
Population: 10,760,000
Language: Portuguese
Currency: Euro

Member: EU, NATO, OECD, OSCE, UN, WEU (associate)
Economy: One of the poorest EU countries, exports include textiles, clothing and shoes.

The green part of the flag represents hope for a free life for all Portuguese. The red field recalls the revolution of 1910-1911, as a result of which the monarchy was abolished. The nautical instrument (armillary sphere) in the center refers to Portugal's great past as a seafaring nation.

Native name: Republica Portuguesa (Portugal)
German: Portugal
French: Portugal
Spanish: Portugal

Romania

Romania
Capital: Bucharest
Area: 238,391 sq. km.
Population: 21,904,000
Language: Romanian
Currency: New Leu

Member: NATO, OSCE, UN, WEU (associate)
Economy: Exports include textiles, clothing, leather goods, and shoes.

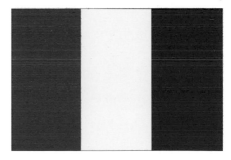

The Romanian tricolor goes back to the main colors of the banners of the medieval principalities of Moldavia (blue), Wallachia (yellow), and Siebenbürgen (red). Today the colors are seen as follows: Blue symbolizes the sky above the golden richness (yellow) of the land; red stands for the people's bravery. The flag was reinstated after the fall of the dictatorial regime in 1989.

Native name: Romania
German: Rumänien
French: Roumanie
Spanish: Rumania

EUROPE

Russia

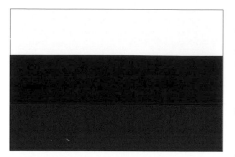

Native name: Rossiyskaya Federatsiya
(Rossiya)
German: Russland
French: Russie
Spanish: Rusia

Russian Federation
Capital: Moscow
Area: 17,098,242 sq. km.
Population: 138,740,000
Language: Russian
Currency: Rubel

Member: G-8, GUS, OSCE, UN
Economy: Over 70% of exports are raw materials and fuels.

The Russian flag was inspired by that of the Netherlands, where Tsar Peter was very impressed on his visit in 1697. He merely changed the order of the stripes. From 1917 to the collapse of the Soviet Union in 1991 the red flag with hammer, sickle, and star was the national flag. Only since 1991 does the white-blue-red tricolor wave again. The 21 autonomous republics of the federation have their own state flags.

San Marino

Native name: Repubblica di San
Marino (San Marino)
German: San Marino
French: Saint Marin
Spanish: San Marino

Republic of San Marino
Capital: San Marino
Area: 61.2 sq. km.
Population: 32,000
Language: Italian
Currency: Euro

Member: OSCE, UN
Economy: Wine, furniture, ceramics, tourism

San Marino is one of the smallest and oldest republics in the world. The white and blue flag goes back to 1797, and the colors are based on the coat of arms, which shows three white castle towers on a blue background. The crown on top is a symbol of independence.

Serbia

Republic of Serbia

Capital: Belgrade
Area: 77,474 sq. km.
Population: 7,311,000
Language: Serbian
Currency: New Dinar

Member: OSCE, UN
Economy: Finished
goods, foods, machines,
apparatus

In 1918 Serbia, Croatia, and Slovenia joined, and, as of 1929, they were called the Kingdom of Yugoslavia. The pan-Slavic colors of the flag, red, blue, and white, stand (as in the French tricolor) for freedom, equality and brotherhood. The Republics of Serbia and Montenegro have their own state flags. In 2006, Montenegro was set up as an independent state and thus separated from Serbia.

Native name: Republika Srbija (Srbija)
German: Serbien
French: Serbie
Spanish: Serbia

Slovakia

Slovak Republic

Capital: Bratislava
Area: 49,034 sq. km.
Population: 5,478,000
Language: Slovakian
Currency: Slovakian
Krone
Member: EU,

NATO,OECD, OSCE, UN,
WEU (associate)
Economy: Exported
are transportation,
machines, among
others, base metals and
mineral products

In 1918 Slovakia became a part of Czechoslovakia under the flag that the Czech Republic now uses. In 1939 a tricolor of white, blue and red was introduced. When Czechoslovakia was dissolved in 1993, the tricolor added the Slovakian arms s to distinguish it from the Russian flag.

Native name: Slovenska Republika
(Slovensko)
German: Slowakei
French: Slovaquie
Spanish: Eslovaquia

EUROPE

Slovenia

Republic of Slovenia
Capital: Ljubljana
Area: 20,253 sq. km.
Population: 2,000,000
Language: Slovenian
Currency: Tolar

Member: EU, NATO,
OSCE, UN, WEU
(associate)
Economy: Machinery,
textiles, chemical
industry

Native name: Republika Slovenija
(Slovenija)
German: Slowenien
French: Slovénie
Spanish: Eslovenia

When the Slovenians rose up against Austrian rule
at Ljubljana in 1848, a flag with three horizontal
stripes of white, blue and red, the pan-Slavic
colors, was hoisted. Since Slovenia's independence
in 1991 the flag has borne the arms with the
highest mountain, Triglav, its foot crossed by two
waves to symbolize the coast or the Sava and
Drava rivers.

Spain

Kingdom of Spain
Capital: Madrid
Area: 505,370 sq. km.
Population: 46,755,000
Languages: Spanish
(regional: Catalan,
Galician, Basque)
Currency: Euro

Member: EU, NATO,
OECD, OSCE, UN, WEU
Economy: 67% of
the gross domestic
product is earned in
services. Partly-made
goods,vehicles, etc. are
exported.

Native name: Reino de España (Espa-
ña)
German: Spanien
French: Espagne

The colors of the Spanish flag come from the coats
of arms of Castile (a golden castle on a red
ground), Aragon (four red posts on a gold
ground), and Navarre (a golden shirt of mail on a
red ground). In the center, on the golden stripe,
is the national coat of arms. The fourth field of
the shield represents the province of Leon.

Sweden

Kingdom of Sweden
Capital: Stockholm
Area: 450,295 sq. km.
Population: 9,089,000
Language: Swedish
Currency: Swedish Krone

Member: EU, OECD,
OSCE, UN, WEU
(observer)
Economy: Machines,
mineral oil, foods,
electrotechnology

The colors of blue and yellow come from the national coat of arms used in the 14th century. The cross form indicates membership in the Nordic peoples. The flag with the horizontal yellow cross on the blue ground has existed for several centuries. It was introduced as the national flag in 1906.

Native name: Konungariket Sverige
   (Sverige)
German: Schweden
French: Suède
Spanish: Suecia

Switzerland

Swiss Confederation
Capital: Bern
Area: 41,285 sq. km.
Population: 7,640,000
Languages: German,
French, Italian,
Raetoromanisch
Currency: Swiss Franc
(Schweizer Franken)

Member: OECD, OSCE,
UN
Economy: This highly
developed industrial
land exports chemicals,
machines, electronics,
instruments, clocks and
watches, etc.

The Swiss national flag is square and shows a white cross on a red ground. This cross stems from the Middle Ages, when many European states used a simple cross on a one-colored ground. The models were the flags of the Holy Roman Empire. In the 13th century the canton of Schwyz already had a flag with a white cross on a red ground.

Native name: Schweiz (German),
   Suisse (French), Svizzera (Italian)
Spanish: Suiza

EUROPE

The Cantons of Switzerland

Aargau
Capital: Aarau
Area: 1,404 sq. km.
Population: 568,671
Language: German

Appenzell Ausserrhoden
Capital: Herisau (seat of govt.)
Area: 243 sq. km.
Population: 52,800
Language: German

Appenzell Innerrhoden
Capital: Appenzell
Area: 173 sq. km.
Population: 15,171
Language: German

Basel-Landschaft
Capital: Liestal
Area: 518 sq. km.
Population: 265,800
Language: German

Basel-Stadt
Capital: Basel
Area: 37 sq. km.
Population: 187,775
Language: German

Bern/Canton de Berne
Capital: Bern
Area: 5,959 sq. km
Population: 956,000
Languages: German, French

Freiburg (Fribourg)
Capital: Freiburg
Area: 1,671 sq. km.
Population: 251,308
Languages: German, French

Geneva (Géneva, Genf)
Capital: Geneva
Area: 282 sq. km.
Population: 441,000
Language: French

Glarus
Capital: Glarus
Area: 685 sq. km.
Population: 38,500
Language: German

Graubünden (Grisons)
Capital: Chur
Area: 7,105 sq. km.
Population: 187,812
Languages: German, Italian, Ratomanisch

The Cantons of Switzerland

Jura
Capital: Delémont
Area: 838 sq. km.
Population: 69,100
Language: French

Luzern (Lucerne)
Capital: Lucerne
Area: 1,493 sq. km.
Population: 354,662
Language: German

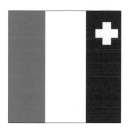

Neuenburg
Capital: Neuchâtel
Area: 803 sq. km.
Population: 167,500
Language: French

St. Gallen
Capital: St. Gallen
Area: 2,026 sq. km.
Population: 457,289
Language: German

Schaffhausen
Capital: Schaffhausen
Area: 298 sq. km.
Population: 73,900
Language: German

Schwyz
Capital: Schwyz
Area: 908 sq. km.
Population: 135,779
Language: German

Solothurn
Capital: Solothurn
Area: 791 sq. km.
Population: 247,400
Language: German

Ticino (Tessin)
Capital: Bellinzona
Area: 2,182 sq. km.
Population: 319,800
Language: Italian

Thurgau
Capital: Frauenfeld
Area: 991 sq. km.
Population: 233,912
Language: German

Unterwalden Nidwalden
Capital: Stans
Area: 276 sq. km.
Population: 39,866
Language: German

Unterwalden Obwalden
Capital: Sarnen
Area: 491 sq. km.
Population: 33,300
Language: German

Uri
Capital: Altdorf
Area: 1,077 sq. km.
Population: 35,100
Language: German

Valais (Wallis)
Capital: Sion (Sitten)
Area: 5,224 sq. km.
Population: 288,800
Languages: French,
German

LIBERTÉ
ET
PATRIE

Vaud (Waadt)
Capital: Lausanne
Area: 3,212 sq. km.
Population: 657,700
Language: French

Zug
Capital: Zug
Area: 239 sq. km.
Population: 104,538
Language: German

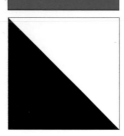

Zürich
Capital: Zürich
Area: 1,729 sq. km.
Population: 1,273,278
Language: German

Ukraine

Ukraine
Capital: Kiev
Area: 603,700 sq. km.
Population: 45,135,000
Languages: Ukrainian,
Russian, minority
languages
Currency: Hryvnya

Member: GUS, OSCE, UN
Economy: Main exports
are iron metals,
minerals and petroleum.

Native name: Ukrayina
German: Ukraine
French: Ukraine
Spanish: Ucrania

The colors of the flag stand for the terrain of the
Ukraine: endless golden wheat fields under a blue
sky. In 1918 the Ukraine was briefly independent
of Russia, but in 1919 it fell under Soviet control
and remained so until 1991. During these years
the flag was banned. Since 1991 the Ukraine has
been independent, and since then the flag has
been allowed again.

United Kingdom

United Kingdom of
Great Britain and
Northern Ireland
Capital: London
Area: 243,610 sq. km.
Population: 62,700,000
Language: English
Currency: Pound

Member: EU, G-8, NATO,
OECD, OSCE, UN, WEU
Economy: Machines and
transport equipment,
chemical products

In the British flag (also called the Union Flag or
Union Jack) the symbols of the parts of the
kingdom are combined: the red straight cross on
white is that of England's patron saint, St. George.
The white diagonal cross on a blue ground is that
of Scotland's patron saint, St. Andrew. The red
diagonal cross on a white ground belongs to
Ireland and St. Patrick. Ireland (later only
Northern Ireland) became part of the kingdom in
1801, and since then the flag has had this form.

Native name: United Kingdom
German: Vereinigtes Königreich Gross-
    britannien und Nordirland
French: Royaume Uni
Spanish: Reuna Unido

Vatican City

The Holy See (State of
Vatican City)
Area: 0.44 sq.km
Population: 832
Languages: Latin,
Italian, German (Swiss
Guard)
Currency: Euro

Member: OSCE
Economy: Postage
stamps and interest on
invested money

Vatican City is the smallest state in the world and
the center of the Roman Catholic Church. The flag
consists of the colors gold and silver, which stand
for those of the keys to heaven which Jesus gave
Peter. On the white band are the keys and over
them the Pope's crown. Since 1929 this flag has
been the state flag of Vatican City.

Native name: Santa Sede (Stato della
    Citta del Vaticano)
German: Vatikanstadt
English: Holy See
French: Saint-siege
Spanish: Santa Sede

MOROCCO

TUNISIA

ALGERIA

LIBYA

EGYPT

WEST SAHARA

CAPE
VERDE

MAURITANIA

SENEGAL

MALI

NIGER

CHAD

SUDAN

ERITREA

GAMBIA

DJIBOUTI

GUINEA-
BISSAU

BURKINA
PASO

GUINEA

NIGERIA

CENTRAL AFRICAN
REPUBLIC

SOUTH
SUDAN

ETHIOPIA

SIERRA
LEONE

IVORY
COAST

SOMALIA

LIBERIA

GHANA

TOGO

BENIN

CAMEROON

EQUATORIAL GUINEA

UGANDA

KENYA

SAO TOMÉ
& PRÍNCIPE

DEMOCRATIC
REPUBLIC
CONGO

RWANDA

SEYCHELLES

GABON

CONGO REPUBLIC

BURUNDI

TANZANIA

COMOROS

ANGOLA

MALAWI

ST. HELENA

ZAMBIA

MOZAMBIQUE

ZIMBABWE

MAURITIUS

NAMIBIA

MADAGASCAR

BOTSWANA

RÉUNION

SWAZILAND

SOUTH AFRICA

LESOTHO

Africa, the Dark Continent, extends 8,000 km from north to south and over 7,600 km from west to east. With 30.3 million square kilometers, it includes one-fifth of the earth's land surface. Over one billion people, nearly 15% of the world's population, live in Africa. 41% of them belong to Islam, 48% are Christians. Africa consists of 54 independent countries recognized by the UN. The largest country is the Sudan, the smallest is Gambia. The largest city is Cairo, with 15 million people.

Africa, because of its size and very difficult access in parts, was the last continent to be colonized and exploited by the Europeans. Only after World War II did many African nations begin to struggle for their sovereignty. Many of the ruling nations granted independence by steps, which happened relatively peacefully in most cases. With independence, most countries decided on new forms for their flags, based on traditional symbols and colors. The pan-African colors of red, yellow, green, and black are seen on many flags; many coats of arms also show weapons or shields reminiscent of African ancestors.

AFRICA

Algeria

People's Democratic
Republic of Algeria
Capital: Algiers
Area: 2,381,741 sq. km.
Population: 34,994,000
Language: Arabic
Currency: Algerian Dinar

Member: AU, OPEC, UN
Economy: Main exports
are petroleum and
hydrocarbons (97%)

The colors of the Algerian flag stand for Islam (green), purity (white), and freedom (red). The star and crescent also stand for Islam. The horns of the moon are unusually long, for long horns are a symbol of good luck in Algeria. In 1925 the flag was first used in demonstrations against the French. Since 1962 it has been the official national flag.

Native name: Al Jumhuriyah al
    Jaza'iriyah ad Dimuqratiyah
    ash Sha'biyah (Al Jaza'ir)
German: Algerien
French: Algérie
Spanish: Argelia

AFRICA

Angola

Republic of Angola

Capital: Luanda
Area: 1,246,700 sq. km.
Population: 13,339,000
Language: Portuguese
Currency: Kwanza

Member: AU, UN
Economy: 72% of
the Angolans work in
agriculture; crude oil and
its products are the main
exports.

Native name: Republica de Angola
    (Angola)
German: Angola
French: Angola
Spanish: Angola

The red strip stands for the blood that the
Angolan people shed during the Portuguese
colonial rule and the subsequent war of liberation.
Black represents the African continent. The half
gear-wheel represents the working class and
industry; the machete represents the farmers and
the battles. The yellow five-pointed star stands for
progress.

Benin

Republic of Benin

Capital: Porto Novo
Area: 112,622 sq. km.
Population: 9,325,000
Language: French
Currency: CFA Franc

Member: AU, UN
Economy: Main exports
are cotton (65%), nuts
and gold.

Native name: Republique du Benin
    (Benin)
German: Benin
Spanish: Benín

The flag shows the pan-African colors of yellow,
red, and green. Here yellow stands for the
savannas in the north, green for palm trees in the
south, and red for the hilly north, but also for the
blood shed by many in the fight for freedom. This
flag flew from 1960 to 1975, was then replaced by
the flag of the people's revolution party, and was
not reintroduced until 1990.

Botswana

Republic of Botswana

Capital: Gaborone
Area: 581,730 sq. km.
Population: 2,065,000
Language: English
Currency: Pula

Member: AU, UN
Economy: Diamonds; 86%
of the exported goods go
to Great Britain

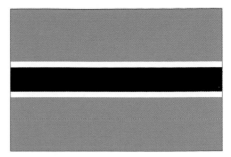

The blue takes up much space in the flag of
Botswana, and that is no surprise: it stands for
the sky that gives rain and for the water, which
the population needs desperately. The black stripe
with narrow white lines symbolizes the black
majority and white minority who live in peaceful
unity.

Native name: Republic of Botswana
(Botswana)
German: Botsuana
French: Botswana
Spanish: Botsuana

Burkina Faso

Burkina Faso

Capital: Ouagadougou
Area: 274,200 sq. km.
Population: 16,751,000
Language: French
Currency: CFA Franc

Member: AU, UN
Economy: Cotton is
the main export; also
animals and animal foods

The flag of Burkina Faso shows the pan-African
colors of red, green and yellow. Red represents the
revolution, green stands for the hope of the
people to attain a revision of the government, and
for the country's natural resources. The star stands
for the leaders of the revolution; its yellow color
warns them not to forget the country's natural
resources.

Native name: Burkina Faso
German: Burkina Faso
Spanish: Burkina Faso

AFRICA

Burundi

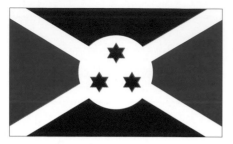

Republic of Burundi
Capital: Bujumbura
Area: 27,834 sq. km.
Population: 10,216,000
Languages: Kirundi, French
Currency: Burundi-Franc

Member: AU, UN
Economy: Exports coffee (50%), also tea and gold.

Native name: Republique du Burundi/
Republika y'u Burundi
(Burundi)
German: Burundi
French: Burundi
Spanish: Burundi

Burundi became independent in 1962 of first German, then Belgian rule. The flag in its present form was introduced in 1967. Red stands for the blood shed in the fight for independence, green for hope, and white for peace. The three stars in the center stand for the Tutsi, Hutu, and Two tribes as well as unity, work, and progress.

Cameroon

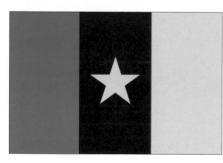

Republic of Cameroon
Capital: Yaoundé
Area: 475,442 sq. km.
Population: 19,711,000
Languages: French, English
Currency: CFA Franc

Member: AU, UN
Economy: Petroleum, cotton, textile fibers, cacao, coffee and aluminum are exported.

Native name: Republique du Cam-
eroun/Republic of Cameroon
(Cameroun/Cameroon)
German: Kamerun
Spanish: Camerún

The pan-African colors of the Cameroon flag are arranged like the French tricolor. The rich vegetation and hope for well-being are expressed in the green and yellow stripes; the red stripe symbolizes the national identity. The star stands for the unity of the land, which consisted of French and British Cameroon until 1961. It was introduced in its present form in 1975.

Cape Verde

Republic of Cape Verde
Capital: Cidade de Praia
Area: 4,036 sq. km.
Population: 516,000
Language: Portuguese
Currency: Cape Verde
Escudo

Member: AU, UN
Economy: Main exports
are clothing and shoes
(89% of total); Portugal
is the main buyer.

Cape Verde became independent of Portugal, which had owned it since the 15th century, in 1975. The blue ground of the flag symbolizes the sky and the ocean, the ten stars represent the ten islands of which the country consists. The white stripes stand for peace and harmony, while the red stripe stands for progress and the efforts that must be made to achieve it.

Native name: Republica de Cabo Verde
(Cabo Verde)
German: Kap Verde
French: Cap-Vert
Spanish: Cabo Verde

Central African Republic

Central African Republic
Capital: Bangui
Area: 622,436 sq. km.
Population: 4,950,000
Languages: Sango,
French
Currency: CFA Franc

Member: AU, UN
Economy: Diamonds,
coffee, cotton and wood

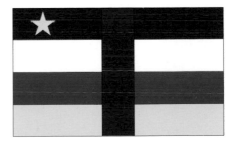

Blue, white, and red are the colors of the France, the former colonial power, and the pan-African colors of green, red and yellow also appear. The combination of colors stands for friendship and partnership between Europe and Africa. The golden star symbolized the country's independence, attained in 1958. The red vertical stripe also stands for the blood of all races and peoples.

Native name: République Centrafri-
caine
English: Central African Republic
Spanish: República Centroafricana

AFRICA
Chad

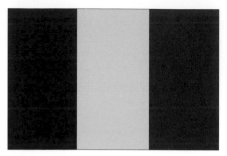

Republic of Chad
Capital: N'Djamena
Area: 1,284,000 sq. km.
Population: 10,759,000
Languages: French, Arabic
Currency: CFA franc

Member: AU, UN
Economy: Cotton and animal products are the main exports.

Native name: Republique du Tchad/
    Jumhuriyat Tshad (Tchad)
German: Tschad
Spanish: Chad

The flag of Chad was influenced by the French tricolor, as the French conquered the land in 1900. The blue stripe symbolizes the sky and the water in the south, yellow is dedicated to the life-giving sun and refers to the desert in the north. Red symbolizes the emotion and dedication of the people that led them to independence in 1960.

Comoros

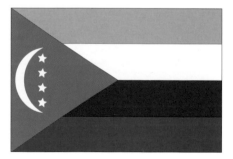

Union of the Comoros
Capital: Moroni
Area: 2,235 sq. km.
Population: 795,000
Languages: Arabic, Comorish, French
Currency: Comorish Franc

Member: AU, UN
Economy: Vanilla, cloves, ylang-ylang

Native name: Udzima wa Komori
    (Comorian); Union des Comores
    (French); Jumhuriyat al
    Qamar al Muttahidah (Arabic)
    (Comores)
German: Komoren
French: Comores
Spanish: Comoras

In 1975, the Comoros became independent of France. Their first flag was red and bore Islamic symbols. With the adoption of a new constitution and a new name, "Union of the Comoros," a new flag was introduced. The green triangle and crescent moon stand for Islam, the four stars and four stripes for the four main islands, Moheli (yellow), Mayotte (white), Anjouan (red) and Grand Comoro (blue).

Democratic Republic of the Congo

Democratic Republic of the Congo
Capital: Kinshasa
Area: 2,344,885 sq. km.
Population: 71,713,000
Language: French
Currency: Congo Franc

Member: AU, UN
Economy: Main exports are diamonds (58%), also crude oil, copper, cobalt and gold

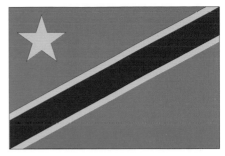

The present national flag of the Democratic Republic of the Congo was introduced on February 18, 2006, after the ratification of the new constitution. It resembles the flag that was valid from 1963 to 1971. The blue ground symbolizes peace, the gold star unity. The red stripe stands for the blood of martyrs and the golden frame for the riches of the land.

Native name: République Démocratique du Congo
German: Demokratische Republik Kongo
Spanish: Républica Democrática del Congo

Republic of the Congo

Republic of the Congo
Capital: Brazzaville
Area: 342,000 sq. km.
Population: 4,244,000
Language: French
Currency: CFA Franc
Member: UN

Economy: Crude oil and wood are the main exports, mainly to mainland China, the Republic of Korea and the United States.

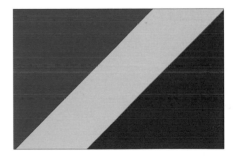

The flag of the Republic of the Congo bears the pan-African colors of red, yellow and green. Green symbolizes agriculture, yellow the mineral wealth, and red stands for independence and recalls that the blood of all races is red. The flag was first introduced in 1959, then again in 1991 after the Marxist government collapsed.

Native name: République du Congo
German: Kongo
Spanish: Congo

51

AFRICA
Djibouti

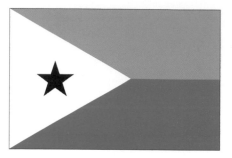

Republic of Djibouti

Capital: Djibouti
Area: 23,200 sq. km.
Population: 757,000
Languages: Arabic, French
Currency: Djibouti Franc

Member: AU, UN
Economy: Main exports are hides, skins and other animal products

Native name: Republique de Djibouti/ Jumhuriyat Jibuti
German: Dschibuti
Spanish: Yibuti

The blue stripe represents the Issa people, the green one the Afar people. These two ethnic groups make up the majority of Djibouti's population. The white triangle is to symbolize the peaceful political togetherness of the two peoples; the star stands for the unity of the people.

Egypt

Arab Republic of Egypt

Capital: Cairo
Area: 1,002,000 sq. km.
Population: 82,080,000
Language: Arabic
Currency: Egyptian Pound

Member: AU, UN
Economy: Main exports are fuels, oils, semi-finished products

Native name: Misr
German: Ägypten
French: Égypte
Spanish: Egipto

Red, white and black are the pan-Arabic colors, and they also stand for the former dynasties of the Hashemites (red), Omayades (white) and Abbasides (black). The revolution of 1952 (which ended the monarchy) is immortalized in the flag; red stands for the sacrificed lives, white for the glowing future, and black for the dark colonial past. The white band bears the eagle of Saladin.

Equatorial Guinea

Republic of Equatorial
Guinea

Capital: Malabo
Area: 28,051 sq. km.
Population: 668,000
Language: Spanish
Currency: CFA Franc

Member: AU, UN
Economy: The main
export is petroleum,
which is exported mainly
to the USA, Spain and
China.

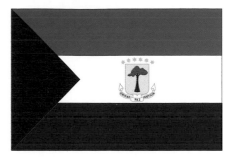

The red stripe of the flag stands for the struggle
for independence, the white for the love of peace,
and the green for the nature and resources of the
country. The blue triangle by the flagpole stands
for the ocean. The arms in the middle of the white
stripe show a kapok tree. The six stars over it
represent the mainland and the five islands.

Native name: Guinea Ecuatorial
German: Äquatorialguinea
French: Guinée équatoriale

Eritrea

State of Eritrea

Capital: Asmara
Area: 117,600 sq. km.
Population: 5,939,000
Languages: Tigrinya,
Arabic

Currency: Nafka
Member: AU, UN
Economy: Foods and live
animals

The three colored triangles of the flag stand for
agricultural wealth (green), marine wealth (blue)
and the blood shed during the fight for
independence (red). The olive plant and the
wreath stand for the peace and prosperity of the
land. In 1993, Eritrea attained independence from
Ethiopia. The present flag has been used since
then.

Native name: Ertra (Tigrinya)
German: Eritrea
French: Érythrée
Spanish: Eritrea

AFRICA
Ethiopia

Democratic Republic of Ethiopia
Capital: Addis Ababa
Area: 1,104,300 sq. km.
Population: 90,874,000
Language: Amharish
Currency: Bir

Member: AU, UN
Economy: Coffee is exported, as are skins and hides, oil seeds, gold and fruit.

Native name: Ityop'iya
German: Äthiopien
French: Éthiopie
Spanish: Etiopía

The colors of the pan-African flag are based on the Ethiopian flag: green, yellow, and red. Green stands for fruitfulness, peace and accomplishment, yellow symbolizes hope, justice and equality, and red stands for work and heroism. The blue color of the emblem stands for peace, the pentagram for unity, and sun rays for equality.

Gabon

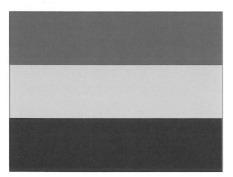

Gabonese Republic
Capital: Libreville
Area: 267,667 sq. km.
Population: 1,577,000
Language: French
Currency: CFA Franc

Member: AU, UN
Economy: Main exports are petroleum, manganese and wood; the USA receives 56%, the European Union 11%.

Native name: Gabon
German: Gabun
French: Gabon
Spanish: Gabón

The flag of Gabon is one of the few black African flags not bearing the pan-African colors. The colors represent the geography of the land: green stands for the vast forests, yellow for the other natural resources, and blue for the ocean. Gabon became independent in 1960 after being a province of French Equatorial Africa.

The Gambia

Republic of the Gambia
Capital: Banjul
Area: 11,295 sq. km.
Population: 1,798,000
Language: English
Currency: Dalasi

Member: AU, UN
Economy: Main exports are peanuts, fish and fish products.

Gambia is the smallest country on the African continent. It became independent of Great Britain in 1965, and the flag was introduced at the same time. The colors are not politically inspired: Red stands for the sun and the savannas, blue for the Gambia River, and green for the forests and landscape. The narrow white stripes stand for unity, peace, and freedom.

Native name: The Gambia
German: Gambia
French: Gambie
Spanish: Gambia

Ghana

Republic of Ghana
Capital: Accra
Area: 238,537 sq. km. \
Population: 24,791,000
Language: English
Currency: Cedi

Member: AU, UN
Economy: Exports gold, cacao and wood, especially to the Netherlands, Great Britain, France, and Germany.

Ghana's flag shows the pan-African colors; red is dedicated to the freedom fighters, yellow stands for the well-being of the country and green represents the fruitful fields and forests. The black star symbolizes the freedom of Africa, The flag was introduced in 1957, when Ghana (Gold Coast) became the first British colony to gain independence.

Native name: Ghana
German: Ghana
French: Ghana
Spanish: Ghana

AFRICA

Guinea

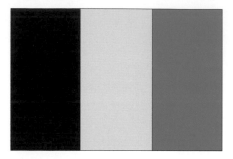

Native name: Guinea
German: Guinea
French: Guinea
Spanish: Guinea

Republic of Guinea

Capital: Conakry
Area: 245,857 sq. km.
Population: 10,601,000
Language: French
Currency: Guinea-Franc

Member: AU, UN
Economy: Aluminum and
aluminum products, 21%
gold

The tricolor of Guinea was introduced in 1958, when the land became independent of France. It had previously been part of French West Africa. The pan-African colors symbolize the self-sacrifice of the people during the fight for freedom (red), the sun and the natural resources (yellow), and the luxuriant vegetation of the land (green).

Guinea-Bissau

Native name: Guiné-Bissau
German: Guinea-Bissau
French: Guinée-Bissau, la Guinée-
        Bissau
Spanish: Guinea-Bissau

Republic of Guinea-
Bissau

Capital: Bissau
Area: 36,125 sq. km.
Population: 1,597,000
Language: Portuguese
Currency: CFA Franc

Member: AU, UN
Economy: Cashew nuts
(96%); main buyer is
India

The flag of Guinea-Bissau was introduced in 1973, when the country became independent of Portugal and a republic was founded. The name of Guinea-Bissau was chosen to differentiate it from its neighbor country. The pan-African colors symbolized the shed blood (red), sun and well-being (yellow) and rich vegetation (green). The black star stands for African unity.

Ivory Coast

Republic of Ivory Coast,
or Côte d'Ivoire

Capital: Yamousoukro
Area: 322, 462 sq. km.
Population: 21,504,000
Language: French
Currency: CFA Franc

Member: AU, UN
Economy: Main exports
are cacao and cacao
products, also petroleum
products, fish, and wood
products.

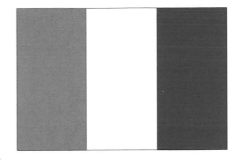

The order of the stripes corresponds to that of the French tricolor. The colors represent the savannas of the north and the people (orange), the rivers, peace and unity (white) and the forests of the south (green). The three colors also represent the motto of the country: Unity, discipline and work.

Native name: Côte d'Ivoire
German: Elfenbeinküste
Spanish: Costa de Marfil

Kenya

Republic of Kenya

Capital: Nairobi
Area: 580,367 sq. km.
Population: 41,071,000
Language: Swahili
Currency: Kenyan
Shilling

Member: AU, UN
Economy: Exports
INCLUDE, among others,
mineral products,
raw materials, tea,
manufactured goods and
coffee

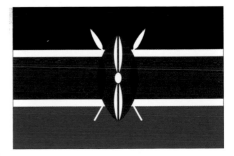

Kenya became independent in 1963 and joined the British Commonwealth in 1964. The colors of the flag are those of the Kenya African National Union (KANU), which came to power with independence. Black stands for the people, red for the blood shed in their fight for freedom, and green for the vegetation. The white stripes stand for unity and peace. The Masai shield and swords recall the ancestors and stand for readiness to defend freedom.

Native name: Kenya
German: Kenia
French: Kenya
Spanish: Kenia

AFRICA

Lesotho

Kingdom of Lesotho
Capital: Maseru
Area: 30,355 sq. km.
Population: 1,925,000
Languages: Sesotho, English

Currency: Loti
Member: AU, UN
Economy: Exports clothing (65%)

Native name: Lesotho
German: Lesotho
French: Lesotho
Spanish: Lesoto

Since October 4, 2006, the 40th anniversary of the country's independence, Lesotho has had a new flag. The colors of blue, white and green stand for rain, peace and well-being and are based on the motto of the country. In the white stripe is a stylized Basotho hat, traditional Lesothish headgear.

Liberia

Republic of Liberia
Capital: Monrovia
Area: 111,369 sq. km.
Population: 3,787,000
Language: English
Currency: Liberian Dollar

Member: AU, UN
Economy: Exports chiefly wood and natural rubber, especially to Germany, Poland and France

Native name: Liberia
German: Liberia
French: Liberia
Spanish: Liberia

Liberia's flag was patterned after the American, and the colony was founded in 1816 to allow former American slaves to return to Africa. The star stands for the light of hope, freedom, and peace that radiates from the country. The blue canton symbolizes the African continent. Blue stands for freedom, white for purity, and red for steadfastness.

Libya

Libya
Capital: Tripoli
Area: 1,775,540 sq. km.
Population: 6,598,000
Language: Arabic
Currency: Libyan Dinar

Member: AU, OPEC, UN
Economy: 95% of exports
are based on crude oil
and natural gas. Italy is
the main buyer.

First introduced in 1951 when the Libyan state was created after World War II, this flag was replaced by a solid green flag by Omar Khadafi in 1977. With his downfall in 2011, the National Transition Council reintroduced the tricolored flag in February 2011, and included it in its Interim Constitutional Declaration. The colors represent the three major regions of Libya: red stands for Fezzan, black for Cyrenaica, and green for Tripolitania; the crescent and star are for Islam.

Native name: al-Dschamahiriyya al-'arabiyya al-libiyya asch-scha'biyya al-ischtirakiyya
German: Libyen
French: Libye
Spanish: Libia

Madagascar

Republic of Madagascar
Capital: Antananarivo
Area: 587,540 sq. km.
Population: 21,926,000
Languages: Malagasy, French
Currency: Ariary

Member: AU, UN
Economy: Main exports
are vanilla (24%) and
crustaceans (18%).

The colors of Madagascar's flag stand for peace and freedom (white), the independence of the country (red), and hope (green). The colors of red and white are also those of the Merina upland folk of pre-colonial times, while green also represents the people of the coasts. Madagascar has been independent since 1960; the flag was introduced in 1958.

Native name: Madagasikara
German: Madagaskar
French: Madagascar
Spanish: Madagascar

AFRICA

Malawi

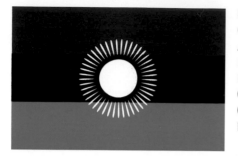

Native name: Malawi (Chichewa)
German: Malawi
French: Malawi
Spanish: Malaui

Republic of Malawi
Capital: Lilongwe
Area: 118,484 sq. km.
Population: 15,879,000
Languages: Chichewa, English
Currency: Malawi-Kwacha

Member: AU, UN
Economy: Tobacco (57%), tea, and sugar are the main exports; the chief buyers are South Africa, the USA, Germany and Japan.

Adopted in July 2010, the new Malawi flag echoes elements of the previous flag, adopted in 1964. but the order of the colors now match the original Pan-African flag and the red rising sun was replaced with this full version in white, symbolizing economic development. The black represents the native people, red the blood shed for freedom, and green the natural bounty of Malawi.

Mali

Native name: Mali
German: Mali
Spanish: Mali

Republic of Mali
Capital: Bamako
Area: 1,240,192 sq. km.
Population: 14.160,000
Language: French
Currency: CFA Franc

Member: AU, UN
Economy: Gold, cotton, and cattle raising

The flag of Mali shows the pan-African colors of green, yellow and red. The green embodies the nature of the land, yellow stands for the natural resources, and red symbolizes the blood shed by the people. Mali had belonged to French West Africa since 1894 as the administrative district of Sudan. Only in 1960 was the Republic of Mali founded.

Mauretania

Islamic Republic of
Mauretania
Capital: Nouakchott   Member: AU, UN
Area: 1,030,700 sq. km. Economy: Iron ore, fish,
Population: 3,282,000   and fish products
Language: Arabic
Currency: Ouguiya

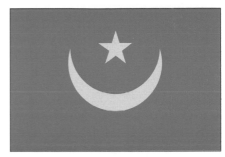

Mauretania was a colony within French West Africa
until 1946, when it became an overseas territory.
In November 1958 the Islamic Republic of
Mauretania was proclaimed. The national flag
shows the Islamic symbols of star and crescent
moon; green is the color of the prophet
Mohammed. Yellow stands for the desert and
natural resources of the country.

Native name: al-Djumhuriyah al-Islu-
    miyah al-Murituniyah
German: Mauretanien
French: Mauritanie
Spanish: Mauritania

Mauritius

Republic of Mauritius
Capital: Port Louis
Area: 2,040 sq. km.   Member: AU, UN
Population: 1,304,000   Economy: Above all,
Language: English,   clothing, sugar cane,
French, Creole Currency: fish and textile yarn are
Mauritius Rupee   exported.

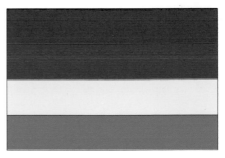

The flag of Mauritius shows four equally wide
horizontal stripes. Red stands for the struggle for
independence, blue for the Indian Ocean, yellow
for the light of freedom, and green for the fruitful
land, sugar cane, and flowers. Mauritius was a
French colony until 1810 and then passed to Great
Britain. The present flag was adopted in 1968
when Mauritius became independent.

Native name: Mauritius
German: Mauritius
French: Maurice
Spanish: Mauricio

AFRICA

Morocco

Kingdom of Morocco
Capital: Rabat
Area: 446,550 sq. km.
Population: 31,968,000
Language: Arabic
Currency: Dirham

Member: UN
Economy: Clothing, hosiery, foods and raw materials

Native name: Al Maghrib
German: Morocco
French: Maroc
Spanish: Marruecos

For over 300 years the current ruling dynasty of the Alavites has used a red flag. Red is also the color of the descendants of Mohammed. The green star in the center stands for wisdom, good fortune and well-being. It was introduced in 1915, and is said to be the seal of King Solomon. The flag was officially confirmed in 1956, when the country became independent. See also Western Sahara, p.72.

Mozambique

Republic of Mozambique
Capital: Maputo
Area: 799,380 sq. km.
Population: 22,949,000
Language: Portuguese
Currency: Metical

Member: AU, UN
Economy: Aluminum and electricity, main buyer is South Africa

Native name: Moçambique
German: Mosambik
French: Mozambique
Spanish: Mozambique

Mozambique became independent of Portugal in 1975. The colors of the flag are based on those of the Frelimo, the ruling political party. Green stands for the agricultural wealth, black for Africa and yellow for the rich natural resources of the land. The white stripes stand for justice and peace. The red triangle recalls the fight against colonialism. The elements of the arms stand for Marxism (star), education (book), watchfulness (machine gun), and agriculture (hoe).

Namibia

Republic of Namibia

Capital: Windhoek
Area: 824,292 sq. km.
Population: 2,148,000
Language: English
Currency: Namibian
Dollar

Member: AU, UN
Economy: Diamonds are
50% of the exports,
bought mainly by South
Africa, Great Britain,
Spain, Japan and
Germany

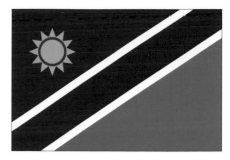

The Namibian flag was introduced in 1990 when
the land became an independent republic. From
1961 until then, it had been administered by
South Africa. Blue stands for the sky and precious
water, red for the working people and their
bravery, and green for the riches of nature. The
golden sun with 12 rays in a blue field symbolizes
life and energy. The white stripes stand for the
peaceful co-existence of all the people in Namibia.

Native name: Namibia
German: Namibia
French: Namibie
Spanish: Namibia

Niger

Republic of Niger

Capital: Niamey
Area: 1,266,700 sq. km.
Population: 16,469,000
Language: French
Currency: CFA Franc

Member: AU, UN
Economy: Mainly
uranium, other ores,
foods, and live animals

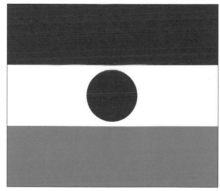

Niger has a horizontal tricolor of orange, white
and green. Orange stands for the Sahara and
savannas, white for purity and innocence and for
the Niger River. Green symbolizes the rain forest
and fruitful soil of the Niger Valley in the south,
as well as for brotherhood. The disc stands for the
sun, but also symbolizes a shield that makes the
people's readiness to defend themselves clear.

Native name: Niger
German: Niger
French: Niger
Spanish: Niger

AFRICA

Nigeria

Federal Republic of Nigeria

Capital: Abuja
Area: 923,768 sq. km.
Population: 155,216,000
Language: English
Currency: Naira

Member: AU, OPEC, UN
Economy: The main export is petroleum (97%); 40% goes to the USA.

Native name: Nigeria
German: Nigeria
French: Nigeria
Spanish: Nigera

The two green stripes stand for the fruitfulness of the land. The white stripe stands for the great Niger River and for unity and peace. The flag was introduced in 1960, when the country became independent. It resulted from a contest which had been announced in 1959, a year before independence.

Réunion

Departement Réunion

Capital: Saint Denis
Area: 2,512 sq. km.
Population: 753,600
Languages: French, Creole, Gujurati
Currency: Euro

Belongs to: France
Economy: Sugar, vanilla, rum and molasses are exported

Native name: Réunion (French)
German: Réunion
Spanish: Reunión

Réunion has been a "Département d'outre-mer" (overseas department) since 1946. It has been French since 1642 and was originally a French penal colony for mutineers. From 1810 to 1814, it was briefly under British rule. Since gaining its present status, the French flag has flown on Réunion. The population is a colorful mixture of French, Africans, and Asians.

Rwanda

Republic of Rwanda

Capital: Kigali
Area: 26,338 sq. km.
Population: 11,370,000
Languages:
Kinyarwanda, French,
English

Currency: Rwandan Franc
Member: AU, UN
Economy: Much coffee
and tea are exported,
mainly to Kenya.

The flag of Rwanda was introduced after the end of the civil war in 2002. The colors represent the Hutu (blue), Tutsi (yellow) and Batwa (green) peoples. The flag symbolizes the peaceful life together under the sun. Blue also stands for the need of enduring peace, yellow for the natural riches, and green for the hope for well-being and use of resources.

Native name: Rwanda (Kinyarwanda)
German: Ruanda
French: Rwanda
Spanish: Ruanda

St. Helena

St. Helena

Capital: Jamestown
Area: 410 sq. km.
Population: 4,647
Language: English
Currency: British Pound

Belongs to: Great Britain
Economy: Chiefly fish
and coffee

St. Helena was uninhabited when discovered by the Portuguese in 1502 or 1503. The Netherlands laid claim to the island in 1633, but there was no settlement until Great Britain's East India Company took possession in 1659. It became a British crown colony in 1834, and has the status of a United Kingdom Overseas Territory. The flag is dark blue and shows the Union Jack in the union plus the coat of arms with a British sailing ship.

Native name: Saint Helena
German: St. Helena
French: Sainte-Hélène
Spanish: Santa Helena

AFRICA
São Tomé and Príncipe

Democratic Republic of
São Tomé and Príncipe
Capital: São Tomé
Area: 964 sq. km.
Population: 179,500
Language: Portuguese
Currency: Dobra

Member: AU, UN
Economy: Main export (80%) is cacao.

Native name: São Tomé e Príncipe
Greman: São Tomé und Príncipe
French: São Tomé-et-Príncipe
Spanish: Santo Tomé y Príncipe

The flag bears the pan-African colors of green, red and yellow. The green stripes stand for the forests and the yellow stripe is for the island soil on which cacao grows. The red triangle is for the blood shed in battle for independence. The two stars on the yellow stripe represent the two islands of São Tomé and Principe. The black color of the stars represents the African people.

Senegal

Republic of Senegal
Capital: Dakar
Area: 196,722 sq. km.
Population: 12,645,000
Language: French
Currency: CFA Franc

Member: AU, UN
Economy: Main export lubricants and chemical products

Native name: Sénégal
German: Senegal
Spanish: Senegal

The flag of Senegal bears the pan-African colors; the design corresponds to the French tricolor. Green stands for hope, but also for the main religions, Islam, Christianity and traditional beliefs. Yellow stands for the richness of nature and the well-being that the people can achieve through work. The red band recalls the struggle for independence, but also stands for life and social justice. The green star in the center symbolizes unity.

Seychelles

Republic of Seychelles

Capital: Victoria
Area: 455 sq. km.
Population: 89,000
Languages: Creole,
English, French
Currency: Seychelles
Rupee

Member: AU, UN
Economy: Fish and fish
products; main buyer is
Great Britain

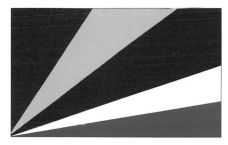

Since independence came in 1976 there have been three different flags on the Seychelles. The five colors of the present flag stand for the two largest parties: blue and white are the Democratic Party colors; red, white and green are those of the Seychelles Peoples United Party (SPUP). Blue also stands for sky and seas, yellow for the sun, red for work, white for harmony and social justice, and green for the environment. The present flag was introduced in 1996.

Native name: Seychelles (English)
German: Seychellen
French: Seychelles
Spanish: Seychelles

Sierra Leone

Republic of Sierra Leone

Capital: Freetown
Area: 71,740 sq. km.
Population: 5,363,000
Language: English
Currency: Leone

Member: AU, UN
Economy: 90% of the
exports are diamonds,
there are also cacao and
coffee.

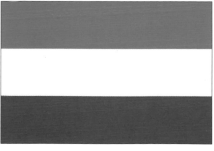

Sierra Leone has been independent of Great Britain since 1961. The colors of its flag come from its arms, developed in London. Green stands for agriculture, natural beauty and mountains. The white stripe symbolizes unity, peace and justice. The blue stripe stands for the ocean and the hope that Freetown, the only natural harbor of the country, will continue to give fine service for foreign trade and economic development.

Native name: Sierra Leone
German: Sierra Leone
French: Sierra Leone
Spanish: Sierra Leone

AFRICA

Somalia

Native name: Soomaaliya
German: Somalia
French: Somalie
Spanish: Somalia

Somalia
Capital: Mogadishu
Area: 637,657 sq. km.
Population: 9,926,000
Language: Somali
Currency: Somalian
Shilling

Member: AU, UN
Economy: Cattle raising,
hides, skins, fruit and
fish

The blue color comes from the United Nations flag.
The white star symbolizes the freedom of Africa
and the African peoples. The five points stand for
the five regions in which the Somali people now
live: Somalia, which was made of the former
British and Italian Somaliland in 1960, plus
Djibouti, Ethiopia and Kenya. The flag was
designed by Mohammed Awale Liban and adopted
in 1954. When the British Somaliland reunited
with Italian Somaliland and became independent
in 1960 the flag became the national emblem.

South Africa

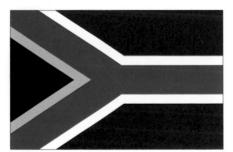

Native name: South Africa
German: Südafrika
French: Afrique du Sud
Spanish: Sudáfrica

Republic of South Africa
Capital: Pretoria
Area: 1,219,090 sq. km.
Population: 49,004,000
Languages: English,
Afrikaans, IsiZulu,
IsiXhosa, isiNdebele,
Sesotho, Setswana,

siSwati, Tshivenda,
Xitsonga
Currency: Rand
Member: AU, UN
Economy: Precious
stones, pearls, metals
and mineral.

The colorful South African flag was introduced in
1994 when Apartheid ended. Yellow, black and
green are the colors of the African National
Congress; red, white and blue are the traditional
colors of the Boer republics. The lying Y stands for
the coming together of the formerly hostile groups
and embodies the hope for progress and a unified
path into the future.

South Sudan

Republic of South Sudan

Capital: Juba

Area: 644,329 sq. km.

Population: 8,260,000

Languages: English, Arabic, & regional languages

Currency: Sudanese Dinar

Economy: Petroleum

After years of fighting that claimed millions of lives, South Sudan gained its independence from Sudan in July 2011, The flag of the new nation has three equal horizontal bands of black (top), red, and green; the red band is edged in white; a blue triangle on the hoist side contains a gold, five-pointed star; black represents the people of South Sudan, red the blood shed in the struggle for freedom, green the verdant land, and blue the waters of the Nile; the gold star represents the unity of the states making up South Sudan

Native name: South Sudan

Sudan

Republic of Sudan

Capital: Khartoum

Area: 1,861,484 sq. km.

Population: 45,048,000

Language: Arabic

Currency: Sudanese Dinar

Member: AU, UN

Economy: Petroleum, meat and live animals

Until 1956 the land was ruled by Egypt and Great Britain; the Republic of Sudan was proclaimed in 1968, and a new flag was introduced in 1970. Red stands for revolution, socialism, and progress, white for light, peace, and optimism, and black stands for Africa. The green triangle at the hoist symbolizes Islam and well-being.

Native name: As-Sudan

German: Sudan

French: Soudan

Spanish: Sudán

AFRICA
Swaziland

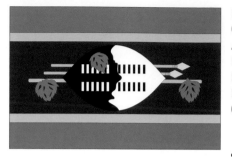

Kingdom of Swaziland
Capital: Mbabane
Area: 17,363 sq. km.
Population: 1,370,000
Languages: Siswati, English
Currency: Lilangeni

Member: AU, UN
Economy: Fruits and fruit concentrates, wood and wood products

Native name: Eswatini
German: Swasiland
French: Swaziland
Spanish: Suazilandia

Swaziland was a British protectorate, ruled by King Mswati III, until 1968. The flag was based on a flag that was given to the Swazi Pioneer Corps of the British Africa Corps by King Sobhuza II in 1941. It was first flown in 1967, when British colonial rule ended, and became official on October 1, 1968. Blue stands for peace, yellow for natural resources. The red central stripe recalls past battles. The Swazi shield stands for the Swazi warriors' readiness to fight.

Tanzania

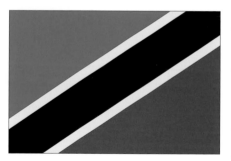

United Republic of Tanzania
Capital: Dar es Salaam
Area: 945,087 sq. km.
Population: 42,747,000
Languages: Swahili, English
Currency: Tanzanian

Shilling
Member: AU, UN
Economy: The main export goods are cashew nuts, coffee, minerals, tobacco and cotton.

Native name: Tanzania (Swahili)
German: Tansania
French: Tanzanie
Spanish: Tanzania

The present-day Tanzania is a union of Tanganyika and Zanzibar formed in 1964. The traditional flag colors of the two lands are united in the flag: Green, yellow, and black represent Tanganyika, blue, black and green Zanzibar. Green stands for the land, black for the people and Africa, blue for the ocean and Zanzibar, and yellow for the mineral wealth in Tanzania.

Togo

Togolese Republic
Capital: Lomé
Area: 56,785 sq. km.
Population: 6,772,000
Languages: French, Ewe, Kabyé
Currency: CFA Franc

Member: AU, UN
Economy: Manufactured goods, fertilizers and mineral raw materials, foods and live animals are exported.

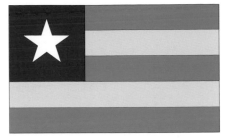

Togo was a German protectorate until 1918, when it was divided between France and Great Britain. It was later administered under UN oversight, becoming autonomous in 1955. In 1960 it became independent and received the name of Togo and adopted the flag. The five-pointed star symbolizes the five regions of the country, green stands for agriculture, yellow for natural resources, red for blood and white for purity and hope.

Native name: République Togolaise (French)
German: Togo
English: Togo
Spanish: Togo

Tunisia

Tunisian Republic
Capital: Tunis
Area: 163,610 sq. km.
Population: 10,629,186
Language: Arabic
Currency: Tunisian Dinar

Member: AU, UN
Economy: Clothing, knitted goods, shoes and oil

Until 1881, Tunisia was part of the Ottoman Empire, whose traditional imperial color was red. The crescent moon and star are traditional symbols of Islam. The Tunisian flag greatly resembles the Turkish flag. The red also stands for the blood shed in the fight for freedom. Introduced in 1831 or 1835, the crescent moon and star in a white circle symbolizes the sun and the unity of the country.

Native name: Tunis
German: Tunesien
French: Tunisie
Spanish: Túnez

AFRICA
Uganda

Republic of Uganda
Capital: Kampala
Area: 241,548 sq. km.
Population: 34,612,250
Languages: Swahili,
English

Currency: Ugandan
Shilling
Member: AU, UN
Economy: Main exports
are coffee, tea and
cotton, 26% going to EU
lands.

Native name: Uganda (English)
German: Uganda
French: Ouganda
Spanish: Uganda

Uganda became independent of Great Britain in 1962. Since then, this three-colored flag with a crane in the center has flown over the land. It is based on the flag of the victorious party (UPC) and, with the addition of the crane, was made the national flag. The colors symbolize Africa and its people (black), the sun (yellow), and the friendship of man (red).

Western Sahara

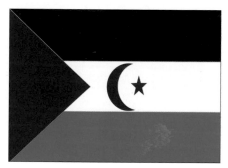

Democratic Arabic
Republic of Sahara
Capital: El-Aujún
Area: 266,001 sq. km.
Population: 507,000
Language: Arabic
Currency: Sahuraui-

Peseta (Moroccan
dirham)
Economy: Chiefly
agrarian; great poverty
prevails.

Former names: Rio de Oro, Saguia el
Hamra, Spanish Sahara
German: Westsahara
French: Sahara occidental
Spanish: Sáhara Occidental

In 1976, the Polisario Front proclaimed a government in exile for Sahrawi Arab Democratic Republic, and this is the Polisario flag. Morocco (p.62) disputes this status and the issue has been before the United Nations since it brokered a cease fire in 1991. The Polisario government was recognized and seated by the Organization of African Unity in 1984. The flag uses the pan-Arabic colors. Red is for the shed blood, black for the colonial rule, white for peace and green for progress and Islam.

Zambia

Republic of Zambia
Capital: Lusaka
Area: 752,614 sq. km.
Population: 13,881,000
Language: English
Currency: Kwacha

Member: AU, UN
Economy: Copper;
main buyers are Great
Britain, South Africa and
Switzerland

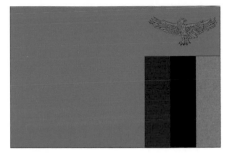

The big green field of the flag symbolizes the
natural wealth of the country. At the outer end
are vertical red, black and orange stripes. They
stand for the fight for freedom (red), the Zambian
people (black), and the country's copper deposits
(orange). The flying eagle symbolizes the will to
freedom and the ability of the people to deal with
all problems.

Native name: Zambia
German: Sambia
French: Zambie
Spanish: Zambia

Zimbabwe

Republic of Zimbabwe
Capital: Harare
Area: 390,757 sq. km.
Population: 12,084,000
Language: English
Currency: Zimbabwe
Dollar

Member: AU, UN
Economy: Tobacco,
flowers, sugar, minerals
and industrial goods

The green stripes of the flag stand for vegetation
and agriculture, the yellow for the mineral wealth,
the red for the blood shed during the fight for
independence. The black stripe represents Africa,
the Dark Continent. The red star symbolizes the
socialistic state philosophy. The "Great Zimbabwe
Bird" is the national emblem.

Native name: Zimbabwe
German: Simbabwe
French: Zimbabwe
Spanish: Zimbabue

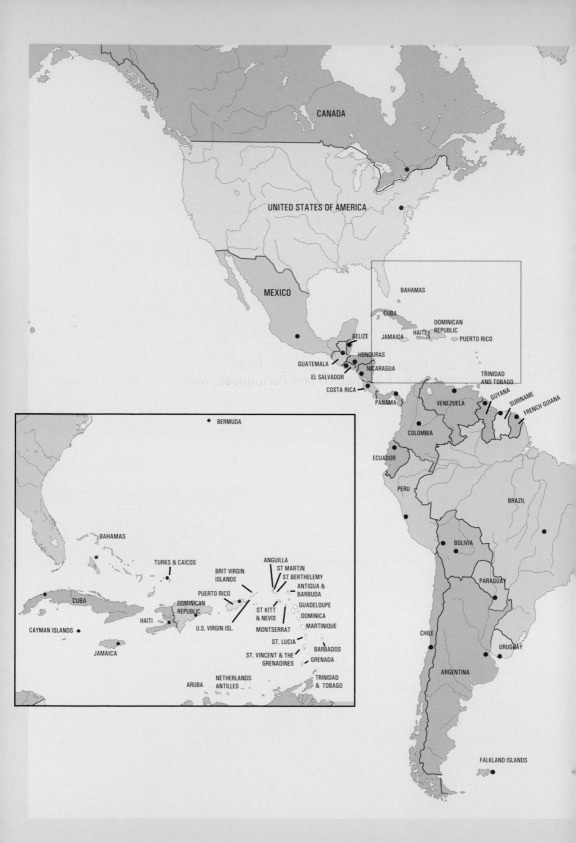

CANADA

UNITED STATES OF AMERICA

MEXICO

BELIZE
HONDURAS
GUATEMALA
EL SALVADOR   NICARAGUA
COSTA RICA
PANAMA

BAHAMAS
CUBA
JAMAICA   HAITI   DOMINICAN
REPUBLIC
PUERTO RICO

TRINIDAD
AND TOBAGO

VENEZUELA   GUYANA
SURINAME
FRENCH GUIANA

COLOMBIA

ECUADOR

PERU

BRAZIL

BOLIVIA

PARAGUAY

CHILE

URUGUAY

ARGENTINA

FALKLAND ISLANDS

BERMUDA

BAHAMAS

TURKS & CAICOS

ANGUILLA
ST MARTIN
ST BERTHELEMY
ANTIGUA &
BARBUDA

BRIT VIRGIN
ISLANDS

PUERTO RICO

CUBA

DOMINICAN
REPUBLIC

HAITI

CAYMAN ISLANDS

JAMAICA

U.S. VIRGIN ISL.

ST KITT
& NEVIS

MONTSERRAT

GUADELOUPE

DOMINICA

MARTINIQUE

ST. LUCIA

ST. VINCENT & THE
GRENADINES

BARBADOS

GRENADA

ARUBA

NETHERLANDS
ANTILLES

TRINIDAD
& TOBAGO

The Americas consist of the two continents of North and South America, linked by the isthmus of Panama, commonly known as Central America. The two continents cover 42 million square kilometers, with 17.8 million sq. km. making up South America, 10 million sq. km. Canada and 9.6 million sq. km. the United States.

The two continents consist of 35 independent states recognized by the UN and many small territories and islands that are administered by other countries. The largest city is Mexico City, with a population of 8.5 million.

After America was discovered by Columbus, settlers from Europe came to it. North America was settled mainly by the Spanish, French, and English, and Central and South America mainly by the Spanish and Portuguese, which has shaped their cultures and languages. During the conquest and settlement Native Americans, the original inhabitants, were decimated and numerous groups completely wiped out.

The most influential and heavily populated country is the United States of America, consisting of 50 states. The flag of the USA, the Stars and Stripes, was the model for numerous other flags.

The countries of Central America look back on colonization and wars of liberation. Many national flags were inspired by the French tricolor.

South America consists of 13 independent countries, the largest being Brazil, the smallest Suriname.

THE AMERICAS

THE AMERICAS
Anguilla

Anguilla
Capital: The Valley
Area: 96 sq. km.
Population: 15,094
Language: English
Currency: East Caribbean Dollar

Belongs to: Great Britain
Economy: Tourism; fish, fruit, salt and rum are exported

Native name: Anguilla
German: Anguilla
French: Anguilla
Spanish: Anguila

Anguilla, since 1650 a British colony consisting of the islands of Anguilla and Sombrero, was proclaimed a republic in 1967. Considerations about a union with St. Kitts and Nevis followed. Since 1980, Anguilla has been a British Overseas Territory with a high degree of self-government. The flag is dark blue, bears the Union Jack in the canton and the coat of arms to its right, consisting of three dolphins that symbolize unity. The light blue stripe stands for the Caribbean.

Antigua and Barbuda

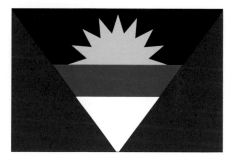

Antigua and Barbuda
Capital: St. John's
Area: 96 sq. km.
Population: 87.884
Language: English
Currency: East Caribbean Dollar

Member: CARICOM, OAS, UN
Economy: Machines, petroleum, manufactured goods

Native name: Antigua and Barbuda
German: Antigua und Barbuda
French: Antiqua-et-Barbuda
Spanish: Antigua y Barbuda

The sun stands for a new era after independence in 1967. The black field symbolizes the African origin of the population. Blue stands for hope, white for sand. The wedge as a whole stands for the English word "Victory" over colonialism. The colors in it represent sun, sea, and sand. The red triangles at the left and right symbolize the energy of the population.

Argentina

Argentine Republic
Capital: Buenos Aires
Area: 2,780,403 sq. km.
Population: 41.769,000
Language: Spanish
Currency: Argentine
Peso

Member: OAS, UN
Economy: mining
products, fuels, foods

Blue and white represent the sky and the snow of the Andes. The flag dates to 1812, and the colors also have political origins. The uniforms of the soldiers of General Belgrano, one of the leaders of the war for independence against Spain, were decorated in blue and white. In 1816 the flag with the three stripes, and in 1818 the "Sun of May," the national symbol, was added, to commemorate the appearance of the sun during a demonstration for independence in May 1810.

Native name: Argentina
German: Argentinien
French: Argentine

Aruba

Aruba
Capital: Oranjestad
Area: 193 sq. km.
Population: 106,100
Languages: Dutch,
Papiamento, Spanish,
English

Currency: Aruban Florin
Belongs to: Netherlands
Economy: Animals
and animal products,
machines and electric
devices are exported

Aruba was a colony of the Netherlands Antilles until 1986. Today it is a constituent country of the Kingdom of the Netherlands, with a parliament, governor and chief of government. It was discovered by the Spaniards in 1499 and has been ruled by the Netherlands since 1636. The flag of Aruba is larkspure or "UN" blue; the two yellow stripes in the lower part symbolize the rainflower, the sun and tourism. Blue stands for the sky and the sea. The star represents Aruba and the four compass points from which settlers came.

Native name: Aruba (Dutch)
German: Aruba
French: Aruba
Spanish: Aruba

THE AMERICAS
The Bahamas

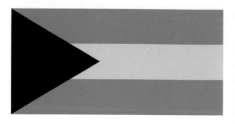

Commonwealth of the
Bahamas
Capital: Nassau
Area: 13,939 sq. km.
Population: 313,000
Language: English
Currency: Bahaman
Dollar

Member: CARICOM, OAS,
UN
Economy: Manufactured
goods, machines,
mineral oils

Native name: The Bahamas
German: Bahamas
French: Bahamas
Spanish: Bahamas

The blue stripes point to the treasures of the sea
that surrounds the Bahamas. The yellow stripe
stands for the resources and the endless sandy
beaches. The triangle at the hoist stands for the
spirit and determination of the population, the
color black reflects the joy of living and strength
of the people. The flag was created in a contest
and introduced in 1973.

Barbados

Barbados
Capital: Bridgetown
Area: 430 sq. km.
Population: 287,000
Language: English
Currency: Barbados
Dollar

Member: CARICOM, OAS,
UN
Economy: Foods, live
animals, petroleum,
chemicals

Native name: Barbados
German: Barbados
French: Barbados
Spanish: Barbados

The blue side stripes stand for the ocean and the
sky, the golden middle stripe for the beaches of
the Caribbean island. The trident recalls Neptune
and shows the people's close contact with the sea.
The fact that the shaft is broken off expresses the
break with the colonial past. The flag was first
hoisted in 1996, when Barbados attained
independence.

Belize

Belize
Capital: Belmopan
Area: 22,965 sq.cm.
Population: 321,000
Language: English
Currency: Belize Dollar

Member: CARICOM, OAS, UN
Economy: Agricultural products, mainly fish and fruit

Blue and white are the colors of the People's United Party, while red is the color of the United Democratic Party. In the middle of the flag is the national coat of arms, surrounded by a wreath of 50 mahogany leaves, recalling the rise to power of the People's United Party in 1950. The arms have existed since 1907, when Belize was still British Honduras.

Native name: Belize
German: Belize
French: Belize
Spanish: Belice

Bermuda

Bermuda
Capital: Hamilton
Area: 54 sq. km.
Population: 65,545
Languages: English, Portuguese
Currency: Bermuda Dollar

Belongs to: Great Britain
Economy: Tourism and finance

Bermuda consists of some 360 islands, only about twenty of which are inhabited. The name came from the Spanish explorer Juan de Bermúdez, who discovered it in 1503. It has been a British colony since 1648 and now is a British Overseas Territory, with self-government, since 1968. It is governed by a governor, head of government and house of representatives. The flag shows the Union Jack in the union, and the coat of arms with a lion holding a shield with a shipwreck.

Native name: Bermuda (English)
German: Bermuda
French: Bermudes
Spanish: Bermudas

THE AMERICAS
Bolivia

Native name: Bolivia (Spanish)
German: Bolivien
English: Bolivia
French: Bolivie

Plurinational State of Bolivia
Capital: Sucre
Administrative: La Paz
Area: 1,098,581 sq. km.
Population: 10,119,000
Languages: Spanish, Quechua, Aimará
Currency: Boliviano
Member: OAS, UN
Economy: Oil and other fuels, soy, soy meal, zinc, tin

The red stripe symbolizes the love of homeland and bravery of the soldiers who fought for independence. The yellow stripe in the middle stands for the rich natural resources of the land and represents the Inca people. Green symbolizes the fruitfulness of the land, as well as hope. The arms show the mountain Potosi, a llama, a breadfruit tree and various weapons and banners.

Brazil

Native name: Brasil
German: Brasilien
English: Brazil
French: Brésil
Spanish: Brasil

Federative Republic of Brazil
Capital: Brasilia
Area: 8,547,404 sq. km.
Population: 203,430,000
Language: Portuguese
Currency: Real
Member: OAS, UN
Economy: Metals and metal products, soy, meat, petroleum

The green color stands for the forests and the wealth of plants. Yellow indicates the wealth of natural resources and minerals. The yellow diamond on a green ground has been on the Brazilian flag since 1822. The constellation of stars in the middle shows the sky over Rio de Janeiro as it was on the day the republic was proclaimed. Every star stands for a federal state, the number of which was last corrected in 1992.

British Virgin Islands

British Virgin Islands
Capital: Road Town
Area: 153 sq. km.
Population: 25,300
Language: English
Currency: U.S. Dollar

Belongs to: Great Britain
Economy: Tourism is most profitable; fruit, rum and fish are exported.

The British Virgin Islands consist of 40 islands, the largest being Tortola, Anegada, Virgin Gorda and Jost Van Dyke. The islands have been British since 1672 and a British colony since 1872. Today they are a British Overseas Territory with self-government, a constitution and a parliament. The flag is dark blue, with the Union Jack in the union. The islands' coat of arms portrays St. Ursula.

Native name: British Virgin Islands
German: Britische Jungferninseln
French: Iles Vierges britanniques
Spanish: Islas Vírgenes Británicas

Canada

Canada
Capital: Ottawa
Area: 9,984,670 sq. km.
Population: 34,000,000
Languages: English, French
Currency: Canadian Dollar

Member: G-8, NAFTA, NATO, OAS, OECD, OSZE, UN
Economy: Machines, automobiles and parts, energy, wood

The Canadian flag with the maple leaf is unmistakable. The maple leaf has been the country's national symbol since the mid-19th century. The red stripes at left and right stand for the Atlantic and Pacific Oceans that border Canada to the east and west. The red color recalls the sacrifices of World War I. The broad white stripe in the middle symbolizes the vast snowy areas in the north. The flag was introduced in 1965.

Native name: Canada (English/French)
German: Kanada
Spanish: Canadá

THE AMERICAS

Cayman Islands

Cayman Islands
Capital: George Town
Area: 259 sq. km.
Population: 51,000
Language: English
Currency: Cayman Dollar

Belongs to: Great Britain
Economy: Tourism and financial services

Native name: Cayman Islands
German: Kaimaninseln
French: Iles Cayman
Spanish: Islas Caima/n

The Cayman Islands consist of Grand Cayman, Cayman Brac, and Little Cayman. They have been British since 1670 and have the status of a British Overseas Territory, with self-government, since 1962. The flag shows the Union Jack in the union, and on the right side the coat of arms that has existed since 1958. It shows three stars for the three islands, a lion, and blue wave lines. The turtle and bananas stand for the flora and fauna.

Chile

Republic of Chile
Capital: Santiago
Area: 756,096 sq. km.
Population: 16,888,000
Language: Spanish
Currency: Chilean Peso

Member: OAS, UN
Economy: Mining, industrial production, fishing, agriculture.

Native name: Chile
German: Chile
French: Chili

The white stripe stands for the snow of the Andes, the red stripe for the blood shed by heroes in the fight for freedom. The blue square symbolizes the sky; the white star is to lead the way to a future of progress. The five points of the star stand for the original five provinces of the country. The flag was introduced when the country became independent in 1817.

Colombia

Republic of Colombia

Capital: Bogota
Area: 1,141,748 sq. km.
Population: 44,724,000
Language: Spanish
Currency: Colombian Peso

Member: CARICOM (observer), OAS, UN
Economy: Petroleum, industrial products, coal, agriculture

The colors of the flag were already used by the Republic of Greater Colombia from 1819 to 1834. That country was divided into Colombia, Venezuela, and Ecuador, and Colombia took over the flag. The yellow stripe symbolizes the golden beaches of Latin America, separated by the ocean (blue) from the bloody colonial power of Spain (red). Today the colors are seen differently; they stand for freedom, justice, and courage.

Native name: Republica de Colombia
German: Kolumbien
French: Colombie

Costa Rica

Republic of Costa Rica

Capital: San José
Area: 51,100 sq. km.
Population: 4,576,000
Language: Spanish
Currency: Costa Rican Colon

Member: OAS, UN
Economy: Electronics, medicinal technology, bananas, pineapple, coffee

The white and blue colors come from the flag of the Central American Federation. The red stripe was added in 1848 at the instigation of the Federation president's wife. She subscribed to the revolutionary ideals of liberty, equality and fraternity. The oval coat of arms shows the three highest mountains of the land amid the blue ocean. Seven stars in the sky indicate the seven provinces.

Native name: Republica de Costa Rica
German: Costa Rica
French: Costa Rica

THE AMERICAS
Cuba

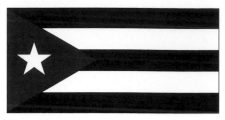

Republic of Cuba
Capital: Havana
Area: 110,860 sq. km.
Population: 11,087,000
Language: Spanish
Currency: Cuban Peso

Member: OAS
(suspended), UN
Economy: Sugar, nickel,
fruit, tobacco

Native name: Republica de Cuba
German: Kuba
French: Cuba

The lone white star, "La Estrella Solitaria," lights the way to freedom. The red triangle at the hoist symbolizes the three basic elements of the republic: liberty, equality and fraternity, the red being for the blood shed in the struggle for independence. The three blue stripes stand for the three provinces of Cuba when it gained its independence. The two white stripes symbolize the purity of the revolution.

Dominica

Commonwealth of
Dominica
Capital: Roseau
Area: 751 sq. km.
Population: 73,000
Language: English
Currency: East Caribbean
Dollar

Member: CARICOM, OAS,
UN
Economy: Soap,
bananas, exported to
Jamaica and Great
Britain

Native name: Dominica
German: Dominica
French: Domonique
Spanish: Domonica

Green stands for the vegetation of the land, the cross symbolizes the Christian faith of the population, the three colors indicate the Trinity. Yellow also stands for the sun, black for the soil and white for the waters. The arms were granted by Great Britain in 1961 and show the Sisserou parrot, the national bird. It is surrounded by ten stars that stand for the ten administrative divisions or parishes.

Dominican Republic

Dominican Republic
Capital: Santo Domingo
Area: 48,422 sq. km.
Population: 9,960,000
Language: Spanish
Currency: Dominican Peso

Member: CARICOM (observer), OAS, UN
Economy: Nickel, raw sugar, cacao, tobacco

The blue rectangles stand for freedom, the red ones recall the courage of the state's founders. The white cross symbolizes Christian salvation as well as the self-sacrifice of the population during the fight for freedom. The coat of arms repeats the flag's colors in the form of a shield and shows a bible open to the Gospel of St. John, a symbol of the Trinitarians who led the fight for freedom against Haiti.

Native name: La Dominicana
German: Dominikanische Republik
French: République dominicaine

Ecuador

Republic of Ecuador
Capital: Quito
Area: 256,370 sq. km.
Population: 15,007,000
Language: Spanish
Currency: U.S. Dollar, Sucre

Member: OAS, UN
Economy: Petroleum, industrial products, bananas, flowers, crabs

The colors of the Ecuadorean flag are based on those of the Gran Colombia that Ecuador joined in 1822, which broke up in 1830. The yellow stripe symbolizes the sun and the natural resources, the blue stripe stands for the sky and sea, and the red stripe for courage and is dedicated to those who shed their blood in the fight for freedom. The arms show the mouth of the Guaya River before the volcano Chimborazo.

Native name: Ecuador
German: Ecuador
French: Équateur

THE AMERICAS
El Salvador

Republic of El Salvador
Capital: San Salvador
Area: 21,041 sq. km.
Population: 6,071,000
Language: Spanish
Currency: El Salvador
Colon

Member: OAS, UN
Economy: Coffee is 1/3
of the total exports

Native name: El Salvador
German: El Salvador
French: Salvador, l'El Salvador

The flag colors of El Salvador go back to the flag of the Federal Republic of Central America, which existed from 1823 to 1838. The two blue stripes symbolize the ocean and Caribbean Sea (although El Salvador is only on the Pacific). The white middle stripe stands for peace. In the middle stripe is the coat of arms, consisting of a triangular shield, representing the judicial, legislative and executive branches. Five volcanoes and five flags stand for the five regions.

Falkland Islands

Falkland Islands
Capital: Stanley
Area: 21,173 sq.km
and 200 small islands
Population: 3,140 and
1,500 British soldiers
Language: English

Currency: Falkland
Pound
Belongs to: Great
Britain
Economy: Raising
animals for meat, skin
and fleece

Native name: Falkland Islands
German: Falkland-Inseln
French: Iles Falkland
Spanish: Islas Malvinas

The Falkland Islands were a British colony since 1838. Since 1985 their status has been a British Overseas Territory. The flag is dark blue, with the Union Jack in the union, plus the arms of the islands. In the upper part of the shield is a ram, indicating the significance of wool. The waved stripes portray the ocean, the ship is the "Desire" on which the discoverers of the islands sailed in 1592. Before 1999 the shield was contained on a white circular background.

French-Guiana

French-Guiana
Capital: Cayenne
Area: 83,534 sq. km.
Population: 173,000
Languages: French, Creole
Currency: Euro

Belongs to: France
Economy: Rum, shrimp, wood, gold and textiles are exported.

The first French settled in the land in 1604, and in 1817 the land became a French possession. In 1946 it was made an Overseas Department of France and gained limited self-government. At the end of the 19th century Brazil made a claim on the area, and the border dispute was ended in favor of French only in 1900. The flag is the French Tricolor.

Native name: Guyane (French)
German: Französisch-Guyana
French: Guyane franç3aise
Spanish: Guayana Francesa

Grenada

Grenada
Capital: St. George's
Area: 344.5 sq. km.
Population: 108,000
Language: English
Currency: East Caribbean Dollar

Member: CARICOM, OAS, UN
Economy: Electronic components, nutmeg

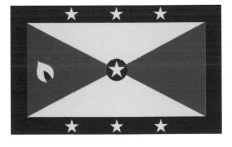

Grenada is also called the spice island, which shows up on the flag. The green triangles stand for the rich vegetation, the nutmeg indicates the island's most important trade goods. The yellow triangles symbolize the island's sunny situation and the people's hearty spirit. The seven stars stand for the seven administrative districts, the red frame for the unity of the people. The flag was introduced on the day of independence in 1974.

Native name: Grenada
German: Grenada
French: Grenade
Spanish: Granada

THE AMERICAS
Guadeloupe

Native name: Guadeloupe (French)
German: Guadeloupe
Spanish: Guadalupe

Guadeloupe
Capital: Basse-Terre
Area: 1,705 sq. km.
Population: 435,000
Languages: French, Creole
Currency: Euro

Belongs to: France, EU
Economy: Tourism is the chief source of income; bananas, sugar and rum are exported.

Guadeloupe has belonged to France since 1635. The land consists of nine inhabited islands. The population is 77% mixed race, 10% Black, 10% Creole and 120,000 Indians. Since 1946 Guadeloupe has been a "Département d'outre-mer" with its own parliament and a prefect in the government. Like the other overseas departments, Guadeloupe uses the French flag. There is also a flag of Guadeloupe that may be flown beside the Tricolor.

Guatemala

Native name: Guatemala
German: Guatemala
French: Guatemala

Republic of Guatemala
Capital: Guatemala
Area: 108,889 sq. km.
Population: 13,800,000
Language: Spanish
Currency: Quetzal

Member: OAS, UN
Economy: Clothing, coffee, bananas, sugar, and petroleum.

The colors of the flag come from those of the Central American Federation. In addition, the blue stripes at the left and right stand for the Atlantic and Pacific Oceans on which Guatemala fronts. Blue also stands for justice and white for righteousness. The arms show guns, bayonets and swords, but also the Quetzal, a rare bird that can survive only in freedom.

Guyana

Cooperative Republic of
Guyana
Capital: Georgetown
Area: 214,969 sq. km.
Population: 745,000
Language: English
Currency: Guyana Dollar

Member: CARICOM, OAS,
UN
Economy: Gold, sugar,
rice, shrimp

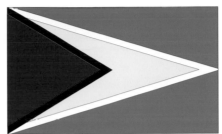

Guyana was a British colony, called British Guiana, until 1966. The flag was introduced in 1966 and had strong color symbolism. Green refers to the agriculture and woodlands, the golden arrow stands for the rich natural resources, the white rim for the waters. The red triangle stands for the people's energy in building an independent nation. The black stripe expresses the resistant power of the people.

Native name: Guyana
German: Guyana
French: Guyana
Spanish: Guyana

Haiti

Republic of Haiti
Capital: Port-au-Prince
Area: 27,750 sq. km.
Population: 9,719,000
Languages: French,
Creole
Currency: Gourde

Member: CARICOM, OAS,
UN
Economy: Manufactured
goods and coffee

The blue stripe stands for the people, the red for the blood shed in the fight for freedom. Haiti declared its freedom from the French occupiers in 1804. The blue-white-red Tricolore flown until then was redesigned without the white stripe, which recalled the occupation. Since 1840 the stripes have been horizontal. The two stripes also symbolize the unity of black and racially mixed people today.

Native name: Haiti (French) /Ayiti
   (Creole)
German: Haiti
Spanish: Haiti

THE AMERICAS

Honduras

Republic of Honduras
Capital: Tegucigalpa
Area: 122,492 sq. km.
Population: 8,144,000
Language: Spanish
Currency: Lempira

Member: OAS, UN
Economy: Shellfish,
coffee, bananas

Native name: Honduras
German: Honduras
French: Honduras

Honduras was a member of the Central American Federation from its founding in 1823 to its dissolution in 1838. The present flag scarcely differs from that of the Federation. The blue stripes symbolize the two oceans which border the country; the white middle stripe stands for the peace in the country. The five stars were added in 1866 and stand for the five founding states: Guatemala, Nicaragua, Honduras, Costa Rica, and El Salvador.

Jamaica

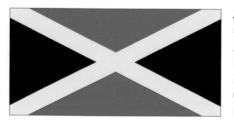

Jamaica
Capital: Kingston
Area: 10,991 sq. km.
Population: 2,868,000
Language: English
Currency: Jamaican
Dollar

Member: CARICOM, OAS,
UN
Economy: Doods, raw
materials, drinks,
tobacco

Native name: Jamaica
German: Jamaika
French: Jamaïque
Spanish: Jamaica

The Jamaican flag was officially introduced on the occasion of the country's independence on August 6, 1962. It was designed by a committee of the Jamaican legislature. Black stands for the difficult past and the challenges that the people still have to overcome. Green symbolizes vegetation and agriculture, but also hope. The golden diagonal cross symbolizes the sun and the country's natural riches.

Mexico

United Mexican States

Capital: Mexico City
Area: 1,953,162 sq. km.
Population: 113,724,000
Language: Spanish
Currency: Mexican Peso

Member: CARICOM
(observer), NAFTA, OAS,
OECD, UN
Economy: Agriculture
and manufacturing

The green stripe at the hoist stands for
independence, the white in the center for the
purity of the (Catholic) faith, and the red stripe at
right represents the equality (of blood) of all races
and people in the country. The arms are based on
the mythology of the Aztecs: Eagle and snake
stand for sun and earth and symbolize the blend
of cosmic powers. The flag has existed in this form
since 1968.

Native name: México
German: Mexiko
France: Mexique

Montserrat

Montserrat

Capital: Brades
Area: 102 sq. km.
Population: 4,482
Language: English
Currency: East Caribbean
Dollar

Belongs to: Great
Britain
Economy: Tourism

Montserrat has been British since 1632. Since
1960 it has been a British Overseas Territory with
self-government. It has a parliament, governor
and chief of the government. The flag is dark blue
with the Union Jack in the union. The arms to the
right show a shield with a woman holding a cross
in her right hand and a harp in her left. It recalls
the Irish immigrants of 1632.

Native name: Montserrat
German: Montserrat
French: Montserrat
Spanish: Montserrat

THE AMERICAS

Netherlands Antilles

Netherlands Antilles
Capital: Willemstad
Area: 800 sq. km.
Population: 180,592
Languages: Dutch, Papiamento, English, Spanish

Currency: Antillean Guilder
Belongs to: Netherlands
Economy: Petroleum products are exported

Native name: Nederlandse Antillen (Dutch)
German: Niederländische Antillen
French: Altilles néerlandaises
Spanish: Antillas Neerlandesas

The Netherlands Antilles consists of five islands: Curaçao is the largest, the others are Bonaire, Saint Maarten (southern part), Saint Eustatius, and Saba. The Antilles have belonged to the Netherlands since 1630 and attained autonomy in 1954. The islands all have their own flags; only Sint Eustatius uses the national flag. White, blue and red are the colors of the Netherlands. The five stars on the blue stripe represent the five islands.

Nicaragua

Republic of Nicaragua
Capital: Managua
Area:120,254 sq. km.
Population: 5,666,000
Language: Spanish
Currency: Cordoba

Member: OAS, UN
Economy: Fruit, meat, coffee, sugar, gold

Native name: Nicaragua
German: Nicaragua
French: Nicaragua

The flag scarcely differs from that of the Central American Federation, which existed from 1821 to 1838. The two blue stripes symbolize the Caribbean Sea and Pacific Ocean, which border Nicaragua. The white stripe stands for peace in the country. The triangular coat of arms on the white stripe stands for equality, the Phyrgian cap for freedom, and the five volcanoes represent the five former states of the Federation.

Panama

Republic of Panama

Capital: Panama
Area: 406,752 sq. km.
Population: 3,460,000
Language: Spanish
Currency: Balboa, US Dollar

Member: OAS, UN
Economy: Fish, shrimp, bananas, pineapple, melons

The colors of the flag are based on those of the country's leading political parties: The Liberals use red, the Conservatives blue; white stands for the peaceful co-existence of the parties. The two stars symbolize the cities of Panama and Colón, the blue also stands for purity, the red for law and order.

Native name: Panamá
German: Panama
French: Panama

Paraguay

Republic of Paraguay

Capital: Asunción
Area: 406,752 sq. km.
Population: 6,459,000
Languages: Spanish, Guarani
Currency: Guarani

Member: OAS, UN
Economy: Fruits for oils, animal fats and oils

Back

Paraguay's flag has an unusual feature, having different emblems on the front and back. Beyond that, the blue stands for good-heartedness, the white for peace and unity, and the red for courage, equality and justice. The star in the coat of arms on the front is a symbol of independence. On the back is the seal of the Treasury Department, a yellow lion below a red Cap of Liberty and the words PAZ Y JUSTICIA (Peace and Justice.

Native name: Paraguay (Spanish)
German: Paraguay
French: Paraguay

THE AMERICAS
Peru

Republic of Peru
Capital: Lima
Area: 1,285,216 sq. km.
Population: 29,249,000
Languages: Spanish,
Quechua, Almara
Currency: New Sol

Member: OAS, UN
Economy: Mining, fish,
clothing

Native name: Perú (Spanish)
German: Peru
French: Pérou

The wide red stripes stand for the blood shed by patriots. The white central stripe symbolizes law and justice. Red was also the color of the Inca kings' tassels, and white was the royal color. The arms show a shield with symbols of the country's animal and plant life. The flag was introduced in 1825.

Puerto Rico

Commonwealth of
Puerto Rico
Capital: San Juan
Area: 8,959 sq. km.
Population: 3,989,000
Languages: English,
Spanish
Currency: US Dollar

Belongs to: USA
Economy: Rum and
drink concentrates,
clothing and electronic
products are exported

Native name: Puerto Rico (English &
    Spanish)
French: Porto Rico

Puerto Rico was ceded to the USA in 1898, after the Spanish-American War. In 1917 the population received US citizenship. Puerto Rico is now a commonwealth, meaning that it is extensively autonomous, as are the states, but the population may not vote in national elections. The flag resembles that of Cuba except that the stripes are red instead of blue, and the triangle is blue instead of red.

St. Barthelemy

Saint Barthelemy
Capital: Gustavia
Area: 21 sq. km.
Population: 7,370
Language: French, English
Currency: Euro

Member: CUPU
Economy: Tourism and duty free commerce

Native name: Saint-Barthelemy
French: Collectivite d'outre mer de Saint-Barthelemy

Christopher Columbus discover the island in 1493 and named it for his brother Bartolomeo. The French settled the island in 1648. In 1784, the French sold the island to Sweden, who renamed the largest town Gustavia and made it a free port. France repurchased the island in 1878 and placed it under the administration of Guadeloupe. In 2003, the populace of the island voted to secede from Guadeloupe and in 2007, the island became a French Overseas Collectivity. It flies the French flag.

St. Kitts and Nevis

Federation of Saint Kitts and Nevis
Capital: Basseterre
Area: 269 sq. km.
Population: 50,300
Language: English
Currency: East Caribbean Dollar

Member: CARICOM, OAS, UN
Economy: Machines and transport equipment, sugar and products

Native name: St. Kitts and Nevis
German: St. Kitts und Nevis
French: Saint-Christophe-et-Niévès; Saint-Christophe-et-Nevis
Spanish: San Cristo/bal y Nieves

The green triangle symbolizes the fruitful soil of the land. The black stripe stands for the African heritage of the population, most of whom are descended from African slaves. The red triangle recalls the islands' troubled past, including slavery and colonial rule. Independence was finally attained in 1983. The stars represent the two islands; the thin yellow stripes stand for the sun.

St. Lucia

Saint Lucia
Capital: Castries
Area: 613.3 sq. km.
Population: 161,000
Language: English
Currency: East Caribbean Dollar

Member: CARICOM ,OAS, UN
Economy: Bananas, beer, clothing

Native name: Saint Lucia
German: Saint Lucia
French: Sainte-Lucie
Spanish: Santa Lucía

The blue background stands for both the sky and the ocean. The triangle symbolizes the island; yellow stands for sunshine and well-being, black for the mainly black population, and the white stripe for the white population. The flag exists in this form since 1979. It was designed by a native artist.

St. Martin & Sint Maarten

Saint Martin

Saint Martin/
Sint Maarten
Capital: Marigot / Philipsburg
Area: 54.4 sq. km./34 sq. km
Population: 30,600 / 37,400

Languages: French, English, Dutch, Spanish
Currency: Euro / Netherlands Antillean guilder
Economy: Tourism

Sint Maarten

Christopher Columbus saw the island in 1493 and claimed it for Spain, but the Dutch occupied the island in 1631 and exploited its salt deposits. Spain reclaimed the island two years later, but eventually abandoned it to the French and Dutch who divided it between them in 1648. Today the northern portion is a French Overseas Collectivity, flying the French Tricolor, and the southern part is an independent nation within the the Kingdom of the Netherlands with its own flag.

St. Vincent and the Grenadines

St. Vincent and the
Grenadines
Capital: Kingstown
Area: 389,3 sq. km.
Population: 104,000
Language: English
Currency: East Caribbean
Dollar

Member: CARICOM, OAS,
UN
Economy: Bananas,
flour, rice

The blue stripe at left stands for the Caribbean
Sea and cloudless sky, yellow symbolizes the
warmth and happiness of the people as well as the
sandy beaches, green stands for the luxuriant
vegetation of the islands and the energy of the
people. The stylized diamonds stand for "V for
victory" and the name of the main island.

Native name: Saint Vincent and the
Grenadines
German: St. Vincent und Grenadinen
French: Saint-Vincent-et-les-Grena-
dines
Spanish: San Vicente y las Grenadinas

Suriname

Republic of Suriname
Capital: Paramaribo
Area: 163,265 sq. km.
Population: 492,000
Language: Dutch
Currency: Suriname
Dollar

Member: CARICOM, OAS,
UN
Economy: Aluminum,
fish and sea creatures

The green stripes symbolize the fruitfulness of the
land and the hope seen by the population in their
independence from the Netherlands, attained in
1975. White stands for peace, freedom and justice.
Red symbolizes love for the land and progress. The
golden star stands for unity and the country's
golden future. The colors of the political parties
are also represented in red and green.

Native name: Suriname
German: Suriname
French: Suriname
Spanish: Surinam

THE AMERICAS
Trinidad and Tobago

Republic of Trinidad and
Tobago
Capital: Port of Spain
Area: 5,128 sq. km.
Population: 1,228,000
Language: English
Currency: Trinidad-and-
Tobago Dollar

Member: CARICOM, OAS,
UN
Economy: Fuels,
lubricants, chemical
products

Native name: Trinidad and Tobago
German: Trinidad und Tobago
French: Trinite'-et-Tobago, Trinidad-
    et-Tobago
Spanish: Trinidad y Tobago

Trinidad and Tobago became independent in 1962,
and the flag has been unchanged since then. The
red color represents the strength of the people,
the black diagonal stripe is the unifying power
embodying the people's solidarity, and also
represents the natural resources of petroleum and
natural gas. The white lines stand for the sea that
links the two main islands, and for the equality of
all peoples.

Turks and Caicos Islands

Turks and Caicos Islands
Capital: Cockburn Town
Area: 430 sq. km.
Population: 45,000
Languages: English,
Creole
Currency: US Dollar

Belongs to: Great
Britain
Economy: Main exports
are aquatic fruits

Native name: Turks and Caicos Islands
    (English)
German: Turks- und Caicos-Inseln
French: Iles Turks-et-Caicos
Spanish: Islas Turcas y Caicos

The Turks and Caicos Islands consist of more than
30 islands, eight of which are inhabited. The
population consists of black and mixed race
people. The status since 1962 is that of a British
Overseas Territory with self-government. The flag
has a dark blue ground with the Union Jack in the
union and the arms of the Turks and Caicos
Islands to the right, consisting of a yellow shield
with a lobster, a snail, and a cactus.

United States

United States of America

Capital: Washington, D.C.
Area: 9,809,155 sq. km.
Population: 290,810,000
Languages: English, Spanish Currency: US Dollar

Member: G-8, NAFTA, NATO, OAS, OECD, OSZE, UN
Economy: Computers, machines, vehicles and parts, chemical products

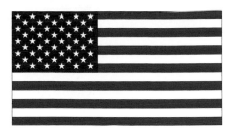

Since 1818 the number of stars in the upper left corner of the flag has equaled the number of states of the USA. The last change took place in 1960 when Hawaii became a state; since then there have been 50 stars. The 13 stripes refer to the founding colonies that federated to form the United States and declared their independence from Great Britain. The white color also stands for purity and red for bravery.

Native name: United States
German: Vereinigte Staaten
French: États-Unis
Spanish: Estados Unidos

Alabama
The Heart of Dixie
Area: 135,775 sq. km.
Capital: Montgomery

Alaska
The Last Frontier
Area: 1,700,138 sq. km.
Capital: Juneau

Arizona
The Grand Canyon State
Area: 295,276 sq. km.
Capital: Phoenix

Arkansas
The Natural State
Area: 137,742 sq. km.
Capital: Little Rock

California
The Golden State
Area: 424,002 sq. km.
Capital: Sacramento

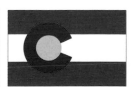

Colorado
The Centennial State
Area: 269,618 sq. km.
Capital: Denver

Connecticut
The Constitution State
Area: 14,358 sq. km.
Capital: Hartford

Delaware
The First State
Area: 6,448 sq. km.
Capital: Dover

THE AMERICAS

Florida
The Sunshine State
Area: 170,314 sq. km.
Capital: Tallahassee

Georgia
The Peach State
Area: 153,952 sq. km.
Capital: Atlanta

Hawaii
The Aloha State
Area: 28,313 sq. km.
Capital: Honolulu

Idaho
The Gem State
Area: 216 456 sq. km.
Capital: Boise City

Illinois
The Prairie State
Area: 150,007 sq. km.
Capital: Springfield

Indiana
The Hoosier State
Area: 94,328 sq. km.
Capital: Indianapolis

Iowa
The Hawkeye State
Area: 145 754 sq. km.
Capital: Des Moines

Kansas
The Sunflower State
Area: 213,111 sq. km.
Capital: Topeka

Kentucky
The Bluegrass State
Area: 104,665 sq. km.
Capital: Frankfort

Louisiana
The Pelican State
Area: 134,275 sq. km.
Capital: Baton Rouge

Maine
The Pine Tree State
Area: 91 653 sq. km.
Capital: Augusta

Maryland
The Old Line State
Area: 32 134 sq. km.
Capital: Annapolis

Massachusetts
The Bay State
Area: 27 337 sq. km.
Capital: Boston

Michigan
The Wolverine State
Area: 250 465 sq. km.
Capital: Lansing

Minnesota
The North Star State
Area: 225 182 sq. km.
Capital: Saint Paul

Mississippi
The Magnolia State
Area: 125 443 sq. km.
Capital: Jackson

Missouri
The Show Me State
Area: 180 546 sq. km.
Capital: Jefferson City

Montana
The Treasure State
Area: 380 850 sq. km.
Capital: Helena

Nebraska
The Cornhusker State
Area: 200 358 sq. km.
Capital: Lincoln

Nevada
The Silver State
Area: 286 367 sq. km.
Capital: Carson City

New Hampshire
The Granite State
Area: 24 219 sq. km.
Capital: Concord

New Jersey
The Garden State
Area: 22 590 sq. km.
Capital: Trenton

New Mexico
The Cactus State
Area: v314 939 sq. km.
Capital: Santa Fé

New York
The Empire State
Area: 141 080 sq. km.
Capital: Albany

North Carolina
The Tar Heel State
Area: 139 397 sq. km.
Capital: Raleigh

North Dakota
The Sioux State
Area: 183 123 sq. km.
Capital: Bismarck

Ohio
The Buckeye State
Area: 116 103 sq. km.
Capital: Columbus

Oklahoma
The Sooner State
Area: 181 048 sq. km.
Capital: Oklahoma City

Oregon
The Beaver State
Area: 254 819 sq. km.
Capital: Salem

Pennsylvania
The Keystone State
Area: 119 291 sq. km.
Capital: Harrisburg

Rhode Island
The Ocean State
Area: 4 002 sq. km.
Capital: Providence

South Carolina
The Palmetto State
Area: 82 902 sq. km.
Capital: Columbia

THE AMERICAS

South Dakota
The Mount Rushmore
State
Area: 199 744 sq. km.
Capital: Pierre

Tennessee
Volunteer State
Area: 109 158 sq. km.
Capital: Nashville

Texas
The Lone Star State
Area: 695 676 sq. km.
Capital: Austin

Utah
The Beehive State
Area: 219 902 sq. km.
Capital: Salt Lake City

Vermont
The Green Mountain
State
Area: 24 903 sq. km.
Capital: Montpelier

Virginia
Old Dominion
Area: 110 792 sq. km.
Capital: Richmond

Washington
The Evergreen State
Area: 184 672 sq. km.
Capital: Olympia

West Virginia
The Mountain State
Area: 62 759 sq. km.
Capital: Charleston

Wisconsin
The Badger State
Area: 169 643 sq. km.
Capital: Madison

Wyoming
The Equality State
Area: 253 349 sq. km.
Capital: Cheyenne

American Virgin Islands

American
Virgin Islands
Capital: Charlotte
Amalie
Area: 352 sq.
km.
Population:
125,000

Languages:
English, Spanish,
Creole
Currency: US
Dollar
Economy:
Tourism

The official status of the Virgin Islands is
that of an unincorporated territory of the
USA. The islands previously belonged to the
British, then the Danes. The flag much
resembles that of the US Army, with a yellow
eagle with outspread wings on a white
ground. It holds an olive branch and three
arrows in its claws. The initials are those of
the Virgin Islands.

Uruguay

Oriental Republic of
Uruguay
Capital: Montevideo
Area: 176,215 sq. km.
Population: 3,308,000
Language: Spanish
Currency: Uruguayan
Peso

Member: OAS, UN
Economy: Deep-frozen
products, leather goods,
grains

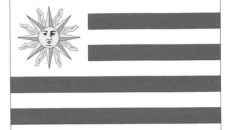

The colors of the flag correspond to those of the
Argentine flag, while the form itself comes from
the American flag. The nine stripes represent the
nine original provinces of the land. Blue stands
for peace, white for freedom. The sun, also called
"Sol de Mayo" (Sun of Freedom), has been the
national emblem since 1815 and symbolizes its
independence.

Native name: Uruguay
German: Uruguay
French" Uruguay

Venezuela

Bolivarian Republic of
Venezuela
Capital: Caracas
Area: 912,050 sq. km.
Population: 27,635,000
Language: Spanish
Currency: Bolivar

Member: CARICOM
(observer), OAS, UN
Economy: Mining, metal
and chemical products

The colors of gold, blue, and red are still
interpreted as in the freedom movement of 1806,
when the flag was first flown in this color
combination. The golden South America is
separated by the blue sea from blood-red Spain.
Blue also stands for freedom, red for courage and
gold for the original federation. The seven stars
represent the seven provinces of the country.

Native name: Venezuela
German: Venezuela
French: Venezuela

TURKEY GEORGIA

ARMENIA KAZAKHSTAN

AZERBAIJAN MONGOLIA NORTH KOREA

LEBANON
ISRAEL
PALESTINIAN SYRIA SOUTH KOREA
TERRITORIES UZBEKISTAN
JORDAN IRAQ KYRGYZSTAN

TURKMENISTAN

KUWAIT TAJIKISTAN

IRAN AFGHANISTAN CHINA

SAUDI ARABIA

QATAR PAKISTAN
BAHRAIN TAIWAN

UNITED ARAB
EMIRATES NEPAL

OMAN BHUTAN

INDIA BANGLADESH
YEMEN MYANMAR

LAOS
VIETNAM

THAILAND
CAMBODIA

BRUNEI

SRI LANKA

MALDIVES MALAYSIA

SINGAPORE

INDONESIA

Asia is the largest continent and contains almost 30% of the earth's land surface. If one adds its islands and inland seas, Asia has an area of 44.2 million square kilometers. Over 3.5 billion people, more than half the world's population, live in Asia. Asia borders on Europe on the west, though the boundary has been variously defined. Sometimes one finds Turkey, Georgia, Armenia, and Azerbaijan ranked as belonging to Europe. In this book they are in the Asian chapter.

This huge continent is often divided into Asia Minor, Central, Northern, Eastern, Southern, and Southeast Asia. In all, the continent consists of 46 independent countries recognized by the UN. Many Near Eastern and Persian Gulf countries express their belonging to the Arabic peoples through the pan-Arabic flag colors of red, white, and black, while the color green stands for Islam. In Eastern and Southeast Asia, Buddhism and Christianity are more strongly represented. Many countries in Southeast Asia were colonized by France and Britain. Only in 1997 was the last British flag lowered, when the Hong Kong became a Special Administrative Region (SAR) of the People's Republic of China.

ASIA

JAPAN

PHILIPPINES

TIMOR-LESTE

ASIA
Afghanistan

Islamic Republic of Afghanistan

Capital: Kabul
Area: 652,225 sq. km.
Population: 29,835,000
Languages: Pashtu, Dari
Currency: Afghani

Member: UN
Economy: Foods and fruits

Native name: Afghanistan (Pashtu), Afghánestân (Dari)
German: Afghanistan
French: Afghanistan
Spanish: Afghanistán

Because of its changing history, Afghanistan has had over 20 different flags in the last hundred years. The present flag goes back to the kingdom of 1931 and has been used again since the fall of the Taliban. Black stands for the dark past, red for the fight for independence, and green for the attainment of independence. The arms symbolize Islam.

Armenia

Republic of Armenia

Capital: Yerevan
Area: 29,743 sq. km.
Population: 2,968,000
Language: Armenian
Currency: Dram

Member: GUS, OSZE, UN
Economy: Precious and semi-precious stones, metals

Native name: Hayastan
German: Armenien
French: Arménie
Spanish: Armenia

The red stripe recalls the long bloody fight for Armenian independence from their Turkish overlords. The blue stripe symbolizes the wide sky over the land and the character of the people, the orange stripe stands for the people's courage and strength. The flag became the state flag after independence from the Soviet Union in 1991.

Azerbaijan

Republic of Azerbaijan
Capital: Baku
Area: 86,600 sq. km.
Population: 8,372,000
Language: Azerbaijani
Currency: Azerbaijan
Manat

Member: UUS, OSZE, UN
Economy: Energy
carriers, foods, pleasure
goods

The blue stripe symbolizes the sky over the land, but also the Azer people. Red stands for freedom and green for the fruitful land. The crescent moon and star (and the color green) are symbols of Islam. The eight points on the star stand for the eight peoples of the country. The flag was reintroduced after the collapse of the Soviet Union in 1991.

Native name: Azärbaycan
German: Aserbaidschan
French: Azerbaídjan
Spanish: Azerbaiyán

Bahrain

Kingdom of Bahrain
Capital: Manama
Area: 760 sq. km.
Population: 1,214,000
Language: Arabic
Currency: Bahrain-Dinar

Member: UN
Economy: Petroleum

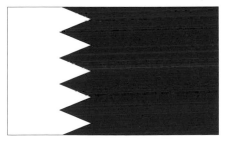

The dominant color of red was originally the color Bahraini Moslems. The white stripe, originally not pointed, was introduced in 1820 as suggested by the British. Until then the flag had been plain red. Since 2002 the line has been defined as having five points, representing the five pillars of Islam.

Native name: Al-Bahrayn
German: Bahrain
French: Bahrein
Spanish: Bahráin

ASIA
Bangladesh

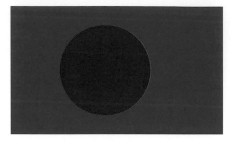

People's Republic of Bangladesh
Capital: Dhaka
Area: 143,998 sq. km.
Population: 158,570,000
Language: Bengali
Currency: Taka

Member: UN
Economy: Clothing, knitted goods, hosiery

Native name: Bangladesh
German: Bangladesch
French: Bangladesh
Spanish: Bangladesh

The green main color of the flag stands for the fruitful land, but also for the Islamic faith to which the majority of the people belong. The red circle symbolizes the bloody battle for independence against the British colonial power in the 1930s. Originally the outlines of the country were shown in yellow in the circle.

Bhutan

Kingdom of Bhutan
Capital: Thimphu
Area: 38,394 sq. km.
Population: 708,000
Language: Dzongkha
Currency: Ngultrum

Member: UN
Economy: Power, wood, calcium carbide

Native name: Druk Yul
German: Bhutan
French: Bhoutan
Spanish: Bután

The left saffron-yellow triangle stands for the secular and religious authority of the king. The red triangle is dedicated to Buddhism. The dragon stands for the name of the country, "Dragon Realm" in Tibetan "Druk yul." The white color of the dragon symbolizes the loyalty of the various peoples and their honesty. The jewels held in the dragon's claws symbolize well-being and perfection.

Brunei

Brunei Darussalam
Capital: Bandar Seri
Begawan Area: 5,765
sq. km.
Population: 402,000
Language: Malayan
Currency: Brunei-Dollar

Member: ASEAN, UN
Economy: Petroleum,
and oil products,
finished goods

In 1906, three governors signed a treaty with the
British government to regulate their mutual rights
and duties: the sultan, whose color is yellow, and
two viziers, whose colors were white and black.
The country's first flag was composed of these
three colors. In 1959 the red emblem of state was
added, symbolizing justice, peace, and Islam.

Native name: Brunei Darussalam
German: Brunei Darussalam
French: Brunei
Spanish: Brunei

Cambodia

Kingdom of Cambodia
Capital: Phnom Penh
Area: 181,135 sq. km.
Population: 14,702,000
Language: Khmer
Currency: Riel

Member: ASEAN, UN
Economy: Textiles and
clothing, rubber and
wood

Blue is the color of the king, red that of the
Khmer people. The central symbol shows a stylized
temple of Angkor Wat, which refers to the glorious
past and tradition of the country. The white color
of the temple stands for belief in the king. The
flag was introduced in 1993.

Native name: Kampuchea
German: Kambodscha
French: Cambodge
Spanish: Camboya

ASIA

China

People's Republic of
China
Capital: Peking (Beijing)   Member: UN
Area: 9,597,961 sq. km.   Economy: Textiles,
Population: office machines,
1,336,718,000   information and
Language: Chinese   electronic technology
Currency: Renmibni Yuan

Native name: Zhonggue
German: China
French: Chine
Spanish: China

Red is both the color of communism and the
traditional color of China and the Han Chinese.
The large star stands for the Communist Party,
while the four small ones represent the four
classes of the people: workers, farmers, bourgeois,
and patriotic capitalists. The flag was introduced
in this form in 1949.

Georgia

Georgia
Capital: Tiflis
Area: 69,700 sq. km.   Member: GUS, OSZE, UN
Population: 4,586,000   Economy: Wine,
Language: Georgian   sugar,copper, gold,
Currency: Lari   scrap metal

Native name: Sak'art'velo
German: Georgien
French: Géorgie
Spanish: Georgia

The flag with the five crosses stems from the
Middle Ages, when it was the flag of the Georgian
kings. As of 1921 Georgia used a variant of the
Soviet flag; in 1990 a black-red-white flag was
introduced, but after a people's revolution in 2004
it was abolished. The present flag symbolizes the
widespread Orthodox faith of the Georgian
population.

India

Republic of India
Capital: New Delhi
Area: 3,287,263 sq. km.
Population:
1,189,173,000
Languages: Hindi,
English, National
languages

Currency: Indian Rupee
Member: UN
Economy: Jewels
and jewelry, textiles,
clothing

The saffron yellow stripe incorporates the people's courage and sacrifice and is also the color of the Hindus and Sikhs. White stands for peace and truth, green for faith in general and Islam. The Ashok Chakra, a 24-spoke wheel, is blue and represents the Laws of Dharma (righteousness).

Native name: Bharat Ganarujya
      (Hindi)
German: Indien
French: Inde
Spanish India (la)

Indonesia

Republic of Indonesia
Capital: Jakarta
Area: 1,904,569 sq. km.
Population: 245,613,000
Language: Indonesian
Currency: Rupiah

Member: ASEAN, OPEC,
UN
Economy: fuels,
oils, machines, foods

The red and white colors were already in use by the 13th century and now serve as the national colors. Red embodies physical life, white stands for spiritual life. Together they stand for the unity of human life in its duality of body and spirit. The flag was adopted in 1945, when the country declared its independence, which it actually attained only in 1949.

Native name: Indonesia
German: Indonesien
French: Indonésie
Spanish: Indonesia

ASIA

Iran

Islamic Republic of Iran
Capital: Teheran
Area: 1,648,000 sq. km.
Population: 77,891,000
Language: Persian
Currency: Rial

Member: OPEC, UN
Economy: Petroleum makes up 80% of the exports

Native name: Îrân
German: Iran
French: Iran
Spanish: Irán

The colors of green, white, and red are the traditional colors of the country, symbolizing Islam, peace, and bravery. The arms in the center consist of four half-moons grouped around a sword. These five elements embody the five basic principles of Islam. The stylized lettering at the edges of the white stripe say "Allah is great" 22 times.

Iraq

Republic of Iraq
Capital: Baghdad
Area: 438,317 sq. km.
Population: 24,700,000
Language: Arabic
Currency: Iraqi Dinar

Member: OPEC, UN
Economy: Crude oil, agriculture, grains, vegetables, dates

Native name: Al Iraq
German: Irak
French: Iraq
Spanish: Iraq

The flag of Iraq consists of the pan-Arabic colors, with red standing for courage in battle, white for dignity and black for the victory of Islam. The green Arabic script centered on the white band is the Takbir (Arabic for "Allah is Great."). This flag was approved in 2008 as temporary replacement for the Ba'athist Saddam-era flag, which had three green stars in addition to the Takbir.

Israel

State of Israel
Capital: Jerusalem
Area: 20,770 sq. km.
Population: 7,473,000
Languages: Hebrew,
Arabic
Currency: New Shekel

Member: UN
Economy: Building
materials, ceramics,
glass, machines,
vehicles

The white field represents the purity of Zionistic ideals. Blue stands for the sky. These two colors and the stripe pattern come from the Jewish prayer shawl. In the center of the white field is the Star of David, a Jewish symbol since the Middle Ages. The flag was introduced as the national flag in 1948.

Native name: Yisra'el (Hebrew)
German: Israel
French: Israël
Spanish: Israel

Japan

Japan
Capital: Tokyo
Area: 377,837 sq. km.
Population: 126,476,000
Language: Japanese
Currency: Yen

Member: G-8, OECD, UN
Economy: Vehicles
and parts, machines,
electrotechnology

The white ground of the flag symbolizes the sky and the purity of the nation. The red sun disc stands for peace and prosperity. The red color symbolizes righteousness and clear understanding in Japan. The sun is an ancient symbol in Japan, whose former emperors saw themselves as direct descendants of the sun god.

Native name: Nihon, Nippon
German: Japan
French: Japon
Spanish: Japón

ASIA

Jordan

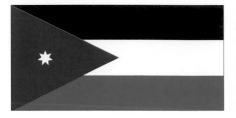

Hashemite Kingdom of Jordan

Capital: Amman
Area: 89,342 sq. km.
Population: 6,508,000
Language: Arabic
Currency: Jordanian Dinar

Member: UN
Economy: Clothing, chemical products, raw materials

Native name: Al-Urdun
German: Jordanien
French: Jordanie
Spanish: Jordania

Each color represents one of the country's families of caliphs. Black stands for the Abbasids, white for the Omajjads, green for the Fatimids and for Mohammed, and red for the Hashemites, from whom the modern kings are presumably descended. The white star symbolizes the first seven verses of the Koran.

Kazakhstan

Republic of Kazakhstan

Capital: Astana
Area: 2,724,900 sq. km.
LanguageL Kazakh
Population: 15,522,000
Currency: Tenge

Member: GUS, OSZE, UN
Economy: Petroleum, natural gas, metals, foods

Native name: Qazaqstan Respublikasy
German: Kasachstan
French: Kazakhstan
Spanish: Kazajistán

Blue stands for the Kazakh people, for peace and plenty, and for the endless sky that spreads over the great land. The sun and the eagle under it express the Kazakh people's love for freedom and their ideals. The yellow design refers to the renowned ornamental art used in making carpets. The flag was introduced in 1992.

Korea (North)

Democratic People's
Republic of Korea

Capital: Pyongyang
Area: 120,538 sq. km.
Population: 24,457,000

Language: Korean
Currency: Won
Member: UN
Economy: Foods, live
animals, textiles

Red stands for the communist revolution, blue for
the sovereignty of the state, and white for the
unity of the people, as well as for purity, strength,
and worth. Blue also symbolizes the Sea of Japan
and Yellow Sea, which enclose Korea on two sides.
Until 1948 North and South Korea had the same
flag.

Native name: Choson
German: Nordkorea
France: Corée du Nord
Spanish: Corel del Norte

Korea (South)

Republic of Korea, or
South Korea

Capital: Seoul
Area: 99,720 sq. km.
Population: 48,755,000
Language: Korean
Currency: Won

Member: OECD, UN
Economy: Information
technology, radio, TV,
vehicles

White stands for peace. In the center of the flag
is the ying-yang symbol, standing for the self-
completing opposites of the country (life and
death, man and woman, day and night). The four
groups of lines (trigrams) symbolize the elements:
water, earth, fire, and sky, as well as the four
seasons and four directions.

Native name: Han'guk
German: Südkorea
French: Corée du Sud
Spanish: Corea del Sur

ASIA

Kuwait

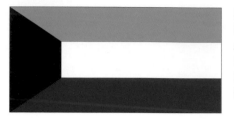

State of Kuwait
Capital: Kuwait City
Area: 17,818 sq. km.
Population: 2,596,000
Language: Arabic
Currency: Kuwaiti Dinar

Member: OPEC, UN
Economy: Petroleum and
its products make up
92% of the exports.

Native name: Al-Kuwait
German: Kuwait
French: Koweït
Spanish: Kuwait

The flag of Kuwait consists of the pan-Arabic colors. Black stands for the battles of the past, green for the fruitful meadows of the country, white for the purity of past and present deeds, and red for the great future prospects of the Arabic peoples. The flag was introduced in 1961.

Kyrgyzstan

Kyrgyz Republic
Capital: Bishkek
Area: 199,951 sq. km.
Population: 5,587,000
Languages: Kyrgyz,
Russian
Currency: Kyrgyz-Som

Member: GUS, OSZE, UN
Economy: Precious
metals, mineral
products, textiles,
leather

Native name: Kyrgyz Respublikasy
(Kyrgyzstan)
German: Kirgisistan
French: Kirghizistan, le Kirghizstan
Spanish: Kirguizistán

The red color honors national hero Manas, who is said to have united the 40 Kyrgyz tribes under a red banner; the 40-rayed sun in the center of the flag also refers to this. Within the sun there is the roof of a yurt, the typical Kyrgyz nomad's tent. Until 1992 Kyrgyzstan was a Soviet republic; since 1992 the country is independent and flies this flag.

Laos

Lao People's Democratic
Republic
Capital: Vientiane
Area: 236,800 sq. km.
Population: 6,477,000
Language: Laotian
Currency: Kip

Member: ASEAN, UN
Economy: Clothing,
electricity, wood and
wood products

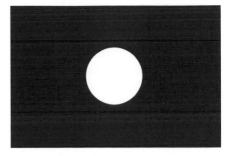

The red border stripes represent the heart and blood of the Laotian people. Blue symbolizes prosperity and a glowing future for the country. The white circle stands for the moon, which is said to bring luck. Laos was a French colony until 1953. The flag was introduced in 1975 when the country became a democratic people's republic.

Native name: Sathalanalat Paxathipa-
    tai Paxaxon Lao
German: Laos
French: Laos
Spanish: Laos

Lebanon

Lebanese Republic
Capital: Beirut
Area: 10,452 sq. km.
Population: 4,143,000
Language: Arabic
Currency: Lebanese
Pound

Member: UN
Economy: Jewelry,
foods, metals

The red stripes stand for the people's self-sacrifice, white symbolizes peace. The tree in the center is a cedar, a symbol of holiness and eternity since ancient times. In the bible, the cedar was already linked with Lebanon. The flag was introduced in its present form on Lebanon's independence in 1943.

Native name: Lubnan
German: Libanon
French: Liban
Spanish: Líbano

ASIA
Malaysia

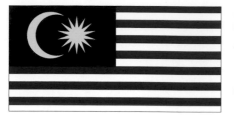

Malaysia
Capital: Kuala Lumpur
Area: 329,733 sq. km.
Population: 28,729,000
Language: Malay
Currency: Ringit

Member: ASEAN, UN
Economy: Electronic components, electric machines, petroleum

Native name: Malaysia
German: Malaysia
French: Malaisie
Spanish: Malasia

The Malaysian flag was inspired by the US flag; the colors are also those of the former colonial power, Great Britain. Red and white are also traditional colors of the country. The blue union stands for the unity of the people, the star and crescent moon are symbols of Islam. The 14 stripes stand for the 13 states and the central government.

Maldives

Republic of Maldives
Capital: Male
Area: 298 sq. km.
Population: 395,000
Language: Divehi
Currency: Rufiyaa

Member: UN
Economy: Fish and fish products, clothing

Native name: Dhivehi Raajje
German: Malediven
French: Maldives
Spanish: Maldivas

Red has been the flag color of the seafaring people of the Maldives since the 19th century. Today it stands for the blood shed by national heroes who fought for independence. The green stands for Islam, and for freedom and progress. The crescent moon is also a symbol of Islam, the faith of the majority of the people.

Mongolia

Mongolia
Capital: Ulaanbaator
Area: 1,564,100 sq. km.
Population: 3,133,000
Language: Mongolian
Currency: Tugrik

Member: UN
Economy: Copper,
textiles, precious metals

Red, blue and yellow are the traditional Mongol colors. Red symbolizes the people's joy of life, blue the sky and eternity, and yellow unending friendship. The symbol on the hoist is called Soyombo and is an old symbol of peace and independence. From 1945 to 1992 the flag also bore the yellow star of Communism.

Native name: Mongol Uls
German: Mongolei
French: Mongolie
Spanish: Mongolia

Myanmar

**Republic of the Union
of Myanmar, or Burma**
Capital: Naypyidaw
Area: 676,552 sq. km.
Population: 54,000,000
Language: Burmese
Currency: Kyat

Member: ASEAN, UN
Economy: Natural gas,
agricultural and forest
products

Burma adopted this flag in 2010 to replace the socialist flag that had been used since 1974. The design consists of three equal horizontal stripes. The yellow (top) stripe represents solidarity, the green (middle) stripe stands for peace, tranquility and green vegetation of the country, and red stripe symbolizes courage and determination. In the center is a five-pointed start that represents the unity of the country. The tri-band colors were used by Burma from 1943-1945, during the Japanese occupation.

Native name: Myanma Naingngandaw
German: Myanmar
French: Birmanie, le Myanmar
Spanish: Birmania, Myanmar

ASIA
Nepal

Federal Democratic
Republic of Nepal
Capital: Katmandu
Area: 147,181 sq. km.
Population: 29,392,000
Language: Nepalese
Currency: Nepalese

Rupee
Member: UN
Economy: Carpets,
textiles, clothing, skins
and hides.

Native name: Nepal
German: Nepal
French: Népal
Spanish: Nepal

The Nepalese flag is the only national flag that is
not square or rectangular. The shape with its two
summits refers to the country's situation in the
mountains. Red is the color of Nepal and its
national flower, the rhododendron. The blue edge
stands for peace. The star and crescent in the
upper half stand for the royal house, the sun in
the lower part for the Rana dynasty. The two parts
symbolize the main religions.

Oman

Sultanate of Oman
Capital: Muscat
Area: 309,500 sq. km.
Population: 3,028,000
Language: Arabic
Currency: Rial Omani

Member: UN
Economy: Petroleum
and natural gas, (80%
of exports)

Native name: Uman
German: Oman
French: Oman
Spanish: Omán

Red is the color of the Charidjite Moslems, white
symbolizes peace and stands for the Imam, the
country's religious leader. Green represents the
fruitful areas and the "green mountain." The state
emblem at the upper left shows two short swords
crossed on a belt and an Arab dagger. The flag
was last changed in 1975.

Pakistan

Islamic Republic of
Pakistan
Capital: Islamabad
Area: 796,095 sq. km.
Population: 187,343,000
Language: Urdu
Currency: Pakistani
Rupee

Member: UN
Economy: Textiles,
knitted goods, bed
linens, clothing

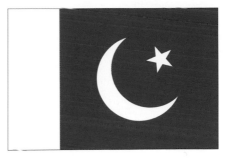

The green color and the star and crescent moon
are symbols of Islam, the dominant religion in
Pakistan. The moon also stands for progress and
the star for knowledge. The white stripe at the
hoist represents the religious minorities in the
country, particularly Hindus. The flag was
introduced in 1947 when Pakistan was founded.

Native name: Pakistan
German: Pakistan
French: Pakistan
Spanish: Pakistán

Palestinian Territories

Palestinian Territories
Capital: Ramallah
Area: 6020 sq. km.
Population: 3,367,000
Languages: Arabic,
Hebrew, English
Currency: Israeli Shekel,
Jordanian Dinar

Economy: Services
lead with 88% of the
economy; exporting is
mainly to Israel.

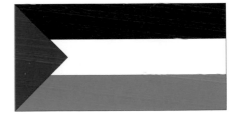

Recognized by 92 nations as the State of Palestine
since its 1988 declaration of independence, the
Palestinian Territories are not recognized bhe U.N.
and the major Western nations, who refer to it as
the Occupied Palestinian Territories. Based on the
Arab League flag, green is for Islam, red for
sacrifice in battle, black for mourning and white
for memory. It was used by the Palestinian
Liberation Organization from 1964 and adopted as
the flag of the State of Palestine in 1988.

Native name: As-Sulta Al-Wataniyya
    (Arabic)
German: Palästinensische Gebiete
French: Autorité palestinienne
Spanish: Autoridad Palestina

ASIA
Philippines

Republic of the
Philippines
Capital: Manila
Area: 300,000 sq. km.
Population: 101,834,000
Language: Filipino
Currency: Philippine
Peso

Member: ASEAN, UN
Economy: Electronics,
electrotechnology,
clothing, machines

Native name: Pilipinas
German: Philippinen
French: Philippines
Spanish: Filipinas

The blue stripe embodies patriotism and idealism, the red stands for bravery. The white triangle symbolizes purity and peace. The three small stars represent the three main regions of the country: Luzon, the Visayan Archipelago, and Mindanao. The sun in the triangle, with its eight rays, stands for the eight provinces that initially opposed Spain.

Qatar

State of Qatar
Capital: Doha
Area: 11,437 sq. km.
Population: 848,000
Language: Arabic
Currency: Qatar Rial

Member: OPEC, UN
Economy: Petroleum,
fertilizers

Native name: Qatar
German: Katar
French: Qatar
Spanish: Qatar

Red and white are the traditional colors of the sheikdoms on the Persian Gulf. But the strong rays of the sun make red cloth darken quickly, and the originally red color was changed to a brownish shade. This color helps differential the Qatar flag from the red of the Bahrain flag. Today the number of points has been fixed at nine, signifying Qatar as the ninth member of the "reconciled emirates" in the wake of the Qatari-British treaty of 1916.

Saudi Arabia

Kingdom of Saudi-
Arabia

Capital: Riyadh
Area: 2,150,000 sq. km.
Population: 26,132,000
Language: Arabic
Currency: Saudi Riyal

Member: OPEC, UN
Economy: Petroleum
and its products,
petrochemicals

Green is the color of Islam and the prophet Mohammed. The sword symbolizes battle and the fighters' obligation to protect the holy cities of Islam: Mecca and Medina. The writing is the Islamic statement of faith: "There is no god but Allah and Mohammed is his prophet."

Native name: Al Arabiyah as-Saudiyah
German: Saudi-Arabien
French: Arabie saoudite
Spanish: Arabia Saudi

Singapore

Republic of Singapore

Capital: Singapore
Area: 682.7 sq. km.
Population: 4,740,000
Languages: Malay,
Tamil, Chinese, English
Currency: Singapore
Dollar

Member: ASEAN, UN
Economy: Fuels, office
machines, chemical
products

The red stripe stands for equality and brotherhood; the white stripe symbolizes the purity of the human spirit and eternal loyalty. The crescent-moon symbolizes the young nation at the beginning of its rise. The five stars symbolize the five ideals that are to be attained: democracy, peace, progress, justice, and equality.

Native name: Singapura (Malay)
German: Singapur
French: Singapour
Spanish: Singapur

ASIA

Sri Lanka

Democratic Socialist Republic of Sri Lanka

Capital: Colombo
Area: 65,610 sq. km.
Population: 21,284,000
Languages: Singhalese, Tamil

Currency: Sri Lanka Rupee
Member: UN
Economy: Consumer goods, machines

Native name: Sri Lanka (Singhalese)
German: Sri Lanka
French: Sri Lanka
Spanish: Sri Lanka

The golden lion is the historical symbol of the state, and its sword expresses authority and power. The leaves in the corners of the red ground recall Buddha. The green stripe represents the Muslims, the orange stripe the Hinduistic Tamils. The yellow edge of the flag honors Buddhism, under the protection of which Sri Lanka stands.

Syria

Syrian Arabic Republic

Capital: Damascus
Area: 185,180 sq. km.
Population: 22,518,000
Language: Arabic

Currency: Syrian Pound
Member: UN
Economy: Fuels, foods, live animals.

Native name: Suriyah
German: Syrien
French: Syrie
Spanish: Siria

The Syrian flag consists of the pan-Arabic colors of red, white, black, and green. Red also stands for revolution, white for a glowing future, black for the sorrows of the past. The two green stars recall the alliance between Syria and Egypt, which lasted only briefly. Sometimes the second star is now attributed to Iraq. The flag has existed since 1980.

Taiwan

Taiwan
Capital: Taipei
Area: 36,306 sq. km.
Population: 23,071,000
Language: Chinese .

Currency: New Taiwan Dollar
Economy: Electronics, metals, textiles, plastics, machines and clocks are exported

After 50 years of Japanese control, Taiwan was governed by the Republic of China after World War II. In 1949, nationalists fled to the island as the communists came into power on the mainland. In 1971 the UN acknowledged the People's Republic of China (PRC) as the sole legal representative of China. The PRC claims ownership of Taiwan. The Taiwanese flag consists of a red ground that expresses sacrifice and brotherhood. The blue union stands for freedom and justice, the white sun represents progress.

Native name: Taiwan
German: Taiwan
French: Taiwan
Spanish: Taiwán

Tajikistan

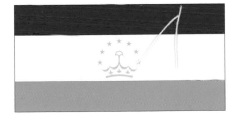

Republic of Tajikistan
Capital: Dushanbe
Area: 143,100 sq. km.
Population: 7,627,000
Language: Tajiki
Currency: Somoni

Member: GUS, OSZE, UN
Economy: Aluminum, cotton, metal products

Long under Russian domination, Tajikistan became part of the USSR in 1925. After the break-up of the Soviet Union in 1991, Tajikistan adopted this new flag in 1992. It took the colors of the republic of the USSR as of 1953 SSR flag which had a red flag with two thin stripes, one white and one green. Today red represents the state, white the cotton production, and green the agriculture. The crown with seven stars symbolizes the independence of the country.

Native name: Todjikiston
German: Tadschikistan
French: Tadjikistan
Spanish: Tayikistán

ASIA
Thailand

Kingdom of Thailand
Capital: Bangkok
Area: 513,115 sq. km.
Population: 66,720,000
Language: Thai
Currency: Baht

Member: ASEAN, UN
Economy: Machines, vehicles, raw materials, foods

Native name: Prathet Thai, Muang
   Thai
German: Thailand
French: Thaïlande
Spanish: Tailandia

In the mid-19th century the flag, then red, was adorned with a white elephant; since 1917 it has borne red, white and blue stripes. Red symbolizes the blood that the Thais would shed for their country, white stands for the purity of the Buddhistic state religion, and blue is the color of the royal house.

Timor-Leste

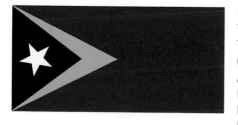

Democratic Republic of Timor-Leste, or East Timor
Capital: Dili
Area: 14,604 sq. km.
Population: 1,178,000
Languages: Tetum, Portuguese

Currency: US Dollar
Member: UN
Economy: Coffee is the chief export.

Native name: Timór Loro Sa'e (Tetum)
   or Timor-Leste (Portuguese)
German: Timor-Leste
French: Timor Oriental
Spanish: Timor Oriental

In 1975 Timor-Leste, often also called East Timor, declared its independence from Portugal. Since then this flag has existed, being slightly changed in 2002. Its symbolism is defined in the country's constitution. Red stands for the wealth, black for the time before independence, yellow for the fight for independence and white for peace. The star symbolizes the light that leads into the future.

Turkey

Republic of Turkey

Capital: Ankara
Area: 779,452 sq. km.
Population: 78,786,000
Language: Turkish
Currency: New Turkish Lira

Member: NATO, OECD, OSZE,
UN, WEU (associate)
Economy: Textiles, clothing, vehicles, iron, vegetables and fruits

Red is the color of the Osmanli or Ottoman Empire, and in 1571 a Turkish fleet used a red flag with three crescent moons in the battle of Lepanto. The crescent moon and star are traditional symbols of Islam. The crescent moon is associated with Osman, the founder of the empire, and stands for happiness and health.

Native name: Türkiye
German: Türkei
French: Turquie
Spanish: Turquía

Turkmenistan

Turkmenistan

Capital: Ashgabat
Area: 488,100 sq. km.
Population: 4,998,000
Language: Turkmenish
Currency: Manat

Member: GUS, OSZE, UN
Economy: Mineral fuels are 86% of the exports.

Green is the color of Islam and the traditional color of the Turkic Tatars. The crescent moon also symbolizes Islam, as well as faith in the future. The stars and the five carpet patterns at the hoist symbolize the five regions of the country. White stands for goodness.

Native name: Turkmenistan
German: Turkmenistan
French: Turkménistan
Spanish: Turkmenistán

ASIA

United Arab Emirates

United Arab Emirates
Capital: Abu Dhabi
Area: 83,600 sq. km.
Population: 5,149,000
Language: Arabic
Currency: Dirham

Member: OPEC, UN
Economy: Petroleum, natural gas

Native name: Al Imarat al Arabiyah al Muttahidah
German: Vereinigte Arabische Emirate
French: Émirats arabes unis
Spanish: Emiratos Árabes Unidos

All the sheikdoms of which the United Arab Emirates was formed in 1971 had red and white as their traditional flag colors. Green was added when the federation was founded and symbolizes fruitfulness and Islam. Black shows the oil wealth of the land. White also stands at present for the country's neutrality.

Uzbekistan

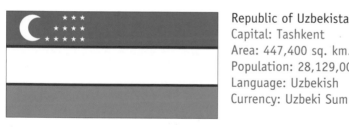

Republic of Uzbekistan
Capital: Tashkent
Area: 447,400 sq. km.
Population: 28,129,000
Language: Uzbekish
Currency: Uzbeki Sum

Member: GUS, OSZE, UN
Economy: Cotton fibers, energy carriers, iron and other metals

Native name: Ozbekiston
German: Usbekistan
French: Ouzbékistan
Spanish: Uzbekistán

The blue stripe symbolizes water and sky, the red-bordered white stripe represents peace and purity, and red lines stand for Islam and nature. The new crescent moon stands for Islam, but also for the existence of a new state; the stars stand for the months of the year and the antiquity of the culture.

Vietnam

Socialist Republic of
Vietnam

Capital: Hanoi
Area: 331,114 sq. km.
Population: 90,549,000
Language: Vietnamese
Currency: Dong

Member: ASEAN, UN
Economy: Crude oil,
textiles clothing, shoes

Red stands for the socialistic revolution and the
sacrifices that the people had to make for it. The
star is a symbol of Communism, and its five points
represent the five groups of people in the socialist
state: workers, farmers, intellectuals, youth, and
soldiers. The flag has flown over the reunited land
since 1976.

Native name: Viet Nam
German: Vietnam
French: Viêt Nam
Spanish: Vietnam

Yemen

Republic of Yemen

Capital: Sanaa
Area: 536,869 sq. km.
Population: 24,123,000
Language: Arabic
Currency: Yemen-Rial

Member: UN
Economy: Petroleum and
its products

The flag of Yemen consists of the pan-Arabic
colors, having the following symbolism here: Red
refers to the revolutions that the north and south
had to endure to become a united state. The
white stripe stands for peace, freedom and
prosperity, the goals of the state. Black recalls the
hard times of division. The flag was introduced in
1990.

Native name: Al Yaman
German: Jemen
French: Yémen
Spanish: Yemen

NORTHERN MARIANA
ISLANDS
GUAM

PALAU

MICRONESIA

MARSHALL ISLANDS

KIRIBATI

NAURU

TUVALU

SOLOMON ISLANDS

TOKELAU

PAPUA NEW GUINEA

WALLIS &
FUTUNA

SAMOA

AMERICAN
SAMOA

VANUATU

FRENCH
POLYNESIA

FIJI

NEW CALEDONIA

TONGA

COOK ISLANDS

AUSTRALIA

PITCAIRN
ISLANDS

NEW ZEALAND

Oceania is composed of over 7,500 Pacific islands, with an area of 8.5 million square kilometers, and a population of over 36.2 million. It consists of 14 independent states recognized by the UN: The Australian mainland (plus Tasmania), New Zealand, the Fiji Islands, Kiribati, Marshall Islands, Micronesia, Nauru, Palau, Papua-New guinea, Solomon Islands, Samoa, Tonga, Tuvalu, and Vanuatu. There are also numerous islands and island groups that are still overseas territories of France, Great Britain, or the USA. The largest country is Australia, the smallest is Nauru. The largest city is Sydney, with 4.15 million Population. Agriculture produces 20% of Australia's economy, with exports including coal, iron ore, gold, sugar, fish, fruit, vegetables and spices.

As varied as the individual states are, so are their populations in terms of origin and ethnic groups. The greater part of the population is of European origin, and there are also Aborigines, Tasmanians, Papuans, and Melanesian peoples living on the many islands. The first English settlement was made in 1788, and the British influence is seen clearly in the flags of Australia and New Zealand, as well as Fiji, Tuvalu, the Cook Islands, and the Pitcairn Islands, which all include the Union Jack.

EASTER
ISLAND

AUSTRALIA/
OCEANIA

AUSTRALIA/OCEANIA

American Samoa

Territory of American Samoa
Capital: Pago Pago
Area: 199 sq. km.
Population: 67,300
Language: Somoan, English, Tongan
Currency: US Dollar

Belongs to: U.S.A.
Economy: Fishing, tourism

Native name: American Somoa

American Samoa is an unincorporated and unorganized territory of the United States. Its flag was adopted in 1960 and represents nation's relationship with the U.S. Blue with a white triangle edged in red that is based on the fly side and extends toward the hoist. The eagle holds the traditional symbols of Samoan chiefs in its talons, a war club, known as a Fa'alaufa'i, and a coconut fiber fly whisk known as a "fue."

Australia

Australia
Capital: Canberra
Area: 7,741.220 sq. km.
Population: 21,766,711
Language: English
Currency: Australian Dollar

Member: OECD, UN
Economy: Ores, metals, coal, fuels

Native name: Australia
German: Australien
French: Australie
Spanish: Australia

The Australian flag bears the Union Jack in its upper left corner, a clear indication of the historic connections with Great Britain. The seven-pointed white star represents the six states and the Northern Territory; the five smaller stars are arranged in the form of the Southern Cross, a widespread symbol in the Southern Hemisphere.

Cook Islands

Cook Islands
Capital: Avarus
Area: 236 sq. km.
Population: 11,124
Languages: English, Maori
Currency: New Zealand Dollar

Economy: Agriculture, light manufacturing, tourism

The Cook Islands are named after Captain Cook, who saw them in 1770. They became a British protectorate in 1888, and were brought under New Zealand's administration by 1900. In 1965 the Cook Island citizens voted for self-government in free association with New Zealand. The blue flag has the Union Jack in the hoist-side quadrant and a large circle of 15 five-pointed stars representing the 15 islands. It was adopted in August, 1979.

Native name: Fiji (English)
German: Fidschi
French: Iles Fidji
Spanish: Fiyi

Easter Island

Easter Island
Capital: Hanga Roa
Area: 164 sq. km.
Population: 5,034
Languages: Spanish, Rapa Nui
Currency: Chilean Peso

Belongs to Chile
Economy: Agriculture, fishing, tourism

Also known as the flag of Rapa Nui or Isla de Pascua, the Easter Island flag is white with a red Reimiro, an Easter Island wood carving worn by the women of the island as a chest piece. It represents a Polynesian canoe, and has a human head at each end.

Native name: Rapa Nui
Spanish: Isla de Pascua

AUSTRALIA/OCEANIA

Fiji

Republic of Fiji
Capital: Suva
Area: 18,376 sq. km.
Population: 883,000
Languages: Fijian, English
Currency: Fiji Dollar

Member: UN
Economy: Drinks, foods, textiles, shoes, tobacco

Native name: Fiji (English)
German: Fidschi
French: Iles Fidji
Spanish: Fiyi

The blue ground symbolizes the Pacific, the Union Jack refers to the historic connection with Great Britain. The arms show a British lion with four white fields under it, separated by the English cross. The fields show sugar cane, a coconut palm, bananas, and a dove of peace.

French Polynesia

French Polynesia
Capital: Papeete
Area: 4,165 sq. km.
Population: 295,000
Languages: French, Tahitian
Currency: CPF-Franc

Belongs to: France
Economy: Coconut oil and cultured pearls are exported

Native name: Polynésie Française
    (French)
German: Französisch-Polynesien
Spanish: Polinesia Francesca

French Polynesia is a self-governing overseas department of France, It consists of five archipelagos: the Society Islands (13 islands), Tuamotu (76 atolls), the Marquesas Islands (10), the Austral Islands (5) and the Gambier Islands (14). The best-known island is Tahiti. The French Tricolor is flown on official occasions, but the red and white native flag is recognized. On the white stripe is an outrigger canoe, with the sun behind it and the sea below. The five stars stand for the five archipelagos.

Guam

Guam
Capital: Hagatna
Area: 594 sq. km.
Population: 183,300
Languages: English,
Chamorro
Currency: US Dollar

Belongs to: USA
Economy: Fish and
sweet potatoes are
exported

Guam, the largest Mariana island, is a non-incorporated territory of the USA and is used as a naval and air base. Until 1898 Guam was Spanish; then it was turned over to the USA. The flag is flown along with that of the USA. The dark blue stands for the Pacific, the oval in the center is shaped like a native catapult stone. It shows a coconut palm that represents perseverance. The boat is a seaworthy canoe, in which fishermen go out to sea.

Native name: Guahan (Chamorro)
German: Guam
French: Guam
Spanish: Guam

Kiribati

Republic of Kiribati
Capital: Tarawa
Area: 810.5 sq. km.
Population: 101,000
Languages: I-Kiribati,
English

Currency: Kiribati Dollar,
Australian Dollar
Member: UN
Economy: Mainly fish
and fish products.

The blue and white wave lines symbolize the Pacific Ocean. The rising sun stands for a glowing future for the country, its 17 rays representing the 16 Gilbert Islands and Banaba. The frigate bird is the national bird of Kiribati and symbolizes strength and freedom. The flag is based on the national arms of 1937 and has existed in this form since independence in 1979.

Native name: Kiribati (English)
German: Kiribati
French: Kiribati
Spanish: Kiribati

Marshall Islands

Republic of the Marshall Islands
Capital: Majuro
Area: 181.3 sq. km.
Population: 67,200
Language: Marshallese, English
Currency: US Dollar
Member: UN
Economy: Fish exported, mainly to the USA

Native name: Marshall Islands
German: Marshallinseln
French: Iles Marshall
Spanish: Islas Marshall

The blue ground symbolizes the Pacific. The orange stripe stands for prosperity and enthusiasm, the white one for the happy life style of the people. Together they also portray the equator. The 24-pointed star stands for the 24 electoral districts; the longer horizontal and vertical rays represent the cultural centers of Majuro, Jaluit, Wotje, and Ebeye. The elongated rays also form a cross that represents Christianity.

Micronesia

Federated States of Micronesia
Capital: Palikir
Area: 700 sq. km.
Population: 107,000
Language: English, Chuukese, Kosrean, Pohnpeian, Yapese,
Ulithian, Woleaian, Nukuoro, Kapingamarangi
Currency: US Dollar
Member: UN
Economy: Fishing and agriculture

Native name: Federated States of Micronesia
German: Mikronesien
French: Micronésie
Spanish: Micronesia

The blue ground color symbolizes the Pacific and is also the blue of the UN flag, under whose administration the islands were for decades. The four stars embody the four island groups: Chuuk, Kosrae, Pohnpei and Yap. Micronesia attained independence in 1979; the flag has flown since 1978.

Nauru

Republic of Nauru
Capital: Yaren
Area: 21.3 sq. km.
Population: 9,350
Languages: Nauruese,
Currency: Australian
Dollar

Member: UN
Economy: Phosphate
mining; subsistence
economy dependent on
Australian aid

The flag reflects the land's situation: The white star stands for Nauru, just south of the Equator (yellow line) surrounded by the Pacific (blue ground). The star has twelve points, one for each twelve indigenous tribes of Nauru. From 1947 to 1968 the island was administered by Australia, Great Britain and New Zealand; then it became independent.

Native name: Nauru
German: Nauru
French: Nauru
Spanish: Nauru

New Caledonia

Territory of New
Caledonia &
Dependencies
Capital: Noumea
Area: 18,575 sq. km.
Population: 256,300
Languages: French,
Melanesian-Polynesian

dialects
Currency: CFP franc
Economy: Nickel mining,
tourism

New Caledonia is an overseas territory of France. it has two official flags, the French Tricolor and, since July 2010, the flag of the independence movement (the Kanak Socialist National Liberation Front). The new flag has three horizontal bands of blue (sky and ocean), red (blood shed in the struggle for independence), and green (the land). The yellow disc represents the sun and the symbol on it is a flèche faitière, an wooden finial or spire that adorns Kanak houses.

Native name: Nouvelle-Calédonie

New Zealand

New Zealand
Capital: Wellington
Area: 270,534 sq. km.
Population: 4,290,000
Languages: English,
Maori

Currency: New Zealand
Dollar
Member: OECD, UN
Economy: Fish, fruit,
animal products, wood

Native name: New Zealand (English)
German: Neuseeland
French: Nouvelle-Zélande
Spanish: Nueva Zelanda

The British Union Jack in the upper left corner
attests to New Zealand's connection with Great
Britain. The four stars (in four different sizes) are
positioned like the Southern Cross constellation
and symbolize the double island's position in the
Pacific. The flag was officially introduced in 1902.

Northern Mariana Islands

Commonwealth of the
Northern MarianaIslands
Capital: Saipan
Area: 464 sq. km.
Population: 46,000
Languages: Philippine
languages, Chinese,
Chamorro, English

Belongs to: USA
Currency: US Dollar
Economy: Tourism,
agriculture, garment
manufacturing

Native name: Northern Mariana
Islands

The Northern Mariana Islands are a commonwealth
in political union with the United States. The flag
has a blue field with a white star superimposed on
a gray latte stone, the traditional foundation
stone in a building. It is surrounded by a wreath.
The blue field represents the ocean, the star is for
the commonwealth, and the stone and floral head
wreath are elements of native culture. It was
adopted in 1981, when the wreath was added.

Palau

Republic of Palau
Capital: Melekeok
Area: 508 sq. km.
Population: 21,000
Languages: Palauish,
English
Currency: US Dollar

Member: UN
Economy: Fish, shellfish
and coconuts

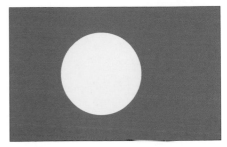

Palau became a republic in 1981, and since then
the flag with the simple design has flown over the
island. Blue naturally symbolizes the sea and sky,
while the golden disc shows the moon, which has
a very special significance. For the natives, the
full moon is considered the optimal time for
activities and undertakings, but stands also for
tranquility, peace and love.

Native name: Belau (Palauish)
German: Palau
French: Belau, Palau
Spanish: Palaos

Papua New Guinea

Independent State of
Papua-New Guinea
Capital: Port Moresby
Area: 462,840 sq. km.
Population: 6,188,000
Languages: English, Tok
Pisin (Pidgin-English),
Hiri Motu

Currency: Kina
Member: UN
Economy: Gold, copper,
petroleum

Red and black are the dominant colors of art and
folklore. The bird of paradise is endemic to the
island of New Guinea and is emblematic of the
tribal culture and stands for the emergence of the
independent Papua-New Guinea. Its feathers also
play a major role in ceremonies, and stand for
peace and freedom. The stylized Southern Cross
indicates the geographical location and the link
with other Pacific countries. The flag was adopted
in 1971.

Native name: Papua New Guinea
(English)
German: Papua-Neuguinea
French: Papouasie-Nouvelle-Guinée
Spanish: Papúa-Nueva Guinea

Pitcairn Islands

Pitcairn Islands
Capital: Adamstown
Area: 47 sq. km.
Population: 48
Languages: English,
Pitkern
Currency: Tala

Belongs to: UK
Economy: Fishing,
subsistance farming,
tourism.

Native name: Pitcairn Islands

An overseas territory of the UK, Pitcairn Island was settled by HMS Bounty mutineers and their Tahitian companions. It was the first Pacific Island to become an English colony (1838). The flag has a blue field with the Union Jack at the upper hoist. The Pitcairn Islander coat of arms is in the outer half of the flag. Green, yellow, and blue represent the island rising from the ocean. The green area has the anchor and bible from the HMS Bounty. At the top is a wheelbarrow and a spring of miro, a local plant.

Samoa

Independent State of Samoa
Capital: Apia
Area: 2,831 sq. km.
Population: 193,000
Languages: Samoan,
English
Currency: Tala

Member: UN
Economy: Fish products,
main buyer is Australia.

Native name: Samoa (English)
German: Samoa
French: Samoa
Spanish: Samoa

The red color stands for courage, blue for freedom, white for purity. The stars in the blue union were borrowed from the flag of New Zealand and represent the Southern Cross constellation, standing for the island state's location in the South Pacific. The present flag was introduced in 1949.

P-T

Solomon Islands

Solomon Islands
Capital: Honiara
Area: 28,896 sq. km.
Population: 572,000
Language: Melanesian pidgin, English
Currency: Solomon Islands Dollar

Member: UN
Economy: Wood, fish, palm oil

The upper triangle of the flag symbolizes the South Pacific, out of which the Solomons rise—the five stars stand for the five main island groups. The green triangle stands for the thick vegetation of the islands. The yellow stripe indicates the sun that shines over all the islands. The flag was introduced in 1977; the Solomons became independent in 1987.

Native name: Solomon Islands
German: Salomonen
French: Iles Salomon
Spanish: Islas Salomón

Tokelau

Tokelau
Area: 12 sq. km.
Population: 1,390
Language: Tokelauan, English
Currency: New Zealand Dollar

Economy: Dependent on New Zealand, sales of copra, postage stamps, souvenir coins, and handicrafts

Tokelau is self-administering territory of New Zealand and until 2009 the New Zealand flag was the official emblem. A new flag was adopted in the fall of 2009. The yellow Tokelauan canoe is on a dark blue field, facing the representation of the Southern Cross constellation. The stars also represent the role of Christianity in the culture and symbolize the country's navigating toward the future. Yellow stands for happiness and peace, and blue represents the ocean.

Native name: Tolelau

AUSTRALIA/OCEANIA

Tonga

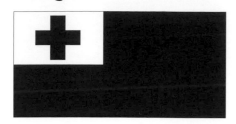

Kingdom of Tonga
Capital: Nuku'alofa
Area: 748 sq. km.
Population: 106,000
Language: Tongan, English
Currency: Pa'anga

Member: UN
Economy: Foods are the main exports

Native name: Tonga
German: Tonga
French: Tonga
Spanish: Tonga

The cross symbolizes Christianity, the faith of the islanders. The red color stands for the blood that Jesus had to shed to save mankind. The white color symbolizes purity. The king was converted by Christian missionaries in 1862. The flag has existed since 1866.

Tuvalu

Tuvalu
Capital: Funafuti
Area: 26 sq. km.
Population: 10,500
Languages: Tuvaluan, English
Currency: Australian Dollar

Member: UN
Economy: Fish is the main export

Native name: Tuvalu (English)
German: Tuvalu
French: Tuvalu
Spanish: Tuvalu

Tuvalu became independent of Great Britain in 1978. Since then the flag has existed in the form shown here. The blue ground represents the Pacific, the nine yellow stars indicate the nine islands of the state, which are actually situated in this form. The Union Jack in the union indicates the link with the former colonial power.

Vanuatu

Republic of Vanuatu
Capital: Port Vila
Area: 12,190 sq. km.
Population: 225,000
Languages: Bislama,
English, French
Currency: Vatu

Member: UN
Economy: Wood and
beef are exported

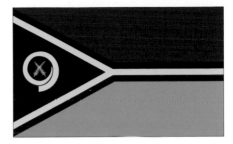

The red part of the flag symbolizes the blood of the people plus the power of their customs. Green stands for the islands and their fruitfulness, black for the population. The yellow Y is a stylized indication of the situation of the islands to each other. Yellow symbolizes peace and the light of Christianity. In the black triangle is the national emblem, a boar's tusk, embodying strength, and two twigs of the namele plant which stands for peace.

Native name: Vanuatu (Bislama)
German: Vanuatu
French: Vanuatu
Spanish: Vanuatu

Wallis and Futuna

Territory of the Wallis
and Futuna Islands
Capital: Mata-Uta
Area: 12,190 sq. km.
Population: 15,400
Languages: Wallisian,
Futunian, French
Currency: CFP francs

Belongs to France
Economy: Subsistence
agriculture, fishing

Wallis and Futuna Islands are an overseas territory of France and their official flag is the French tricolor. A local, unofficial flag is popular and tolerated. It has a red field with 4 white isosceles triangles representing the three kings of the islands and the French administrator. The apexes of the flag point inward and they are at right angles. The French tricolor bordered in white is in the union.

Native name: Wallis and Futuna
French: Territoire des Iles Wallis et
Futuna

INTERNATIONAL

Arab League

Founded: 1945

Purposes: Improving the relations of the member states in terms of politics, culture, society and economy.

Members: 22

Flag: The green color stands for Islam; the white crescent moon in the center is also a symbol of Islam. Over the moon is the name of the league in Arabic lettering, surrounded by a chain that symbolizes unity. A laurel wreath surrounds the chain, standing for peace and security.

European Union - EU

Founded: 1952-1958

Purposes: Economic cooperation, currency union, common foreign and security policy.

Members: 25

Flag: The blue flag with the circle of stars was introduced in 1955 by the council of Europe. The European Union, which replaced the Council, took over the flag in 1986. Each member state was to be represented by a star, but since there are now 25 members, the original form was retained with twelve stars for the 12 founding countries.

International Committee of the Red Cross - ICRC

Founded: 1863

Purposes: Promotion of humanitarian rights, protection and help for war victims, supervision of acceptance of the Geneva Convention.

Members: The committee consists of up to 25 Swiss citizens.

Flag: Since the organization was founded in Switzerland, the colors of the Swiss flag were simply reversed to honor that country. In Muslim countries there has been a similar flag, showing a red crescent moon, since 1876 (Red Cross is called Red Crescent there).

ORGANIZATIONS
North Atlantic Treaty Organization - NATO

Founded: 1949

Purposes: NATO was founded in Washington
in 1949 by twelve West European and North
American states as a security pact. It promotes
political, economic, and military cooperation to
maintain peace and overcome crises.

Members: 26

Flag: The NATO flag was introduced in 1953. The
blue ground stands for the Atlantic Ocean, the
circle for unity and the points of the compass
rose for peace, the main goal of the member
countries.

International Olympic Committee - IOC

This flag, known all over the world, symbolizes the
Olympic movement and the Olympic Games. It was
designed by a Frenchman, Pierre de Courbetin, in
1914. The white ground stands for peaceful and
brotherly relations of the people with each other
and fairness in competition. Each colored ring
stands for a continent: Blue for Europe, black for
Africa, red for America, yellow for Asia and green
for Australia.

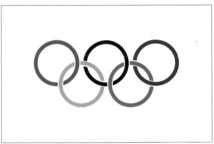

United Nations - UN

Founded: 1945

Purposes: Preservation of world peace, respect
for human rights, international cooperation
for economic, cultural, social, humanitarian
and environmental goals. The UN is the world's
largest and most influential organization.

Flag: The UN flag was introduced in 1947. It is
light blue and shows a stylized world map,
framed by olive branches. Blue and the branches
stand for world peace.

Glossary

badge: A family, city or national coat of arms, such as a shield

banner: A flag hung from a horizontal staff.

bicolor: A two-colored flag, its field divided equally into two horizontal, vertical or diagonal parts.

burgee: A small triangular flag, usually with a swallowtail fly, used by ships.

canton: The upper left (hoist) corner of a flag, separate from the field, and sometimes called the "union."

charge: a figure or symbol on the field of a flag

coat of arms: The emblem of a family, state or country. Most countries have a coat of arms as well as a national flag.

dipping a flag: An international sign of respect of merchant ships for warships; partially lowering the flag one or more times.

dressed ship: A ship decorated with signal flags and burgees.

field: The background or predominant color of a flag.

fimbriation: a narrow edging of color separating two other colors

flag: A piece of fabric, usually rectangular, with a symbolic design representing a nation or other organization, or used as a signaling device.

flag raising: The hoisting of a flag in the morning and lowering at sunset, involving expressions of honor.

floating cross: A cross whose bars do not extend to the edges.

fly: The end of a flag not attached to the mast. In pictures this end is always on the right.

hoist: The edge of the flag closest to the mast or flagpole.

jack: small flag designating a nationality flown from the bow of ship while in port

mast: A wooden, metal or fiberglass staff on which flags are hoisted.

merchant flag: The flag that shows the nationality of merchant and private ships.

Pan-African colors: Green, yellow and red. They go back to the Ethiopian flag..

Pan-Arabic colors: Black, white, green and red. They go back to the Jordanian flag.

Pan-Slavic colors: White, blue and red. They are based on the Russian flag.

pennant: A flag that tapers to a small end, often used at sea.

St. Andrew's cross: A diagonal cross usually extending to the edges of the flag.

St. George's cross: A central cross made of a horizontal and a vertical bar, extending to the edge of the flag.

Scandinavian cross: A cross placed off-center in the direction of the hoist.

state flag: A decorated version of a national flag, used only for service purposes.

tricolor: The French flag, or any other flag divided horizontally or vertically into three equally large parts.

union: *see canton*

Union Jack: The national flag of Great Britain, with the crosses of St. George, St. Andrew and St. Patrick.

Vexillology: The science of flags and flag information.